HOUGHTON MIFFLIN HARCOURT

Comprehensive Language and Literacy Guide

Consultant
Irene C. Fountas

Grade 4

Copyright © 2011 by Houghton Mifflin Harcourt Publishing Company

All rights reserved. No part of this work may be reproduced or transmitted in any form or by any means, electronic or mechanical, including photocopying or recording, or by any information storage and retrieval system, without the prior written permission of the copyright owner unless such copying is expressly permitted by federal copyright law. Requests for permission to make copies of any part of the work should be addressed to Houghton Mifflin Harcourt Publishing Company, Attn: Contracts, Copyrights, and Licensing, 9400 South Park Center Loop, Orlando, Florida 32819.

Printed in the U.S.A.

ISBN 13: 978-0-547-24114-2
ISBN 10: 0-547-24114-3

3 4 5 6 7 8 9 10   0877   18 17 16 15 14 13 12 11 10

If you have received these materials as examination copies free of charge, Houghton Mifflin Harcourt Publishing Company retains title to the materials and they may not be resold. Resale of examination copies is strictly prohibited.

Possession of this publication in print format does not entitle users to convert this publication, or any portion of it, into electronic format.

Comprehensive Language and Literacy Guide

A Readers' Workshop Approach

Introduction: What Are Effective Instructional Practices in Literacy? 1

- Whole-Group Teaching 2
- Small-Group Teaching 4
- Independent Literacy Work 6

Planning for Comprehensive Language and Literacy Instruction 8

Whole-Group Lessons 39

- Interactive Read-Aloud/Shared Reading
- Reading Minilessons

Teaching Genre 101

Appendix 112

- Leveled Readers Database 112
- Literature Discussion: Suggested Trade Book Titles 122
- Professional Bibliography 126

Introduction

What Are Effective Instructional Practices in Literacy?

Your goal in literacy teaching is to bring each student from where he is to as far as you can take him in a school year, with the clear goal of helping each student develop the competencies of proficiency at the level. Proficient readers and writers not only think deeply and critically about texts but also develop a love of reading. The roots of lifelong literacy begin with a rich foundation in the elementary school.

The **Comprehensive Language and Literacy Guide** provides a structure for organizing your literacy teaching, linking understandings across the language and literacy framework, and building a strong foundation of reading strategies and skills. On the pages that follow, you will find an overview of how to use this guide along with your *Journeys* materials in three different instructional contexts: Whole-Group Teaching, Small-Group Teaching, and Independent Literacy Work.

WHOLE GROUP
Interactive Read-Aloud/Shared Reading
(heterogeneous)

WHOLE GROUP
Reading Minilesson
(heterogeneous)

SMALL GROUP
Guided Reading
(temporary homogeneous)

SMALL GROUP
Literature Discussion
(heterogeneous)

INDEPENDENT
Independent Reading, Reader's Notebook, Literacy Work

Whole-Group Teaching

👤 TEACHER'S ROLE

- Engage students in thinking deeply about texts.
- Provide a learning environment in which students feel comfortable sharing their thinking with each other.
- Prepare explicit lessons that are tailored to students' needs.
- Provide a model of phrased, fluent reading in interactive read-aloud.
- Prompt students with comments and questions at planned stopping points to promote active thinking in interactive read-aloud/shared reading.
- Provide explicit teaching of critical literacy concepts in reading minilessons.
- Expose students to a wide variety of genres, authors, and topics.
- Monitor students' understanding to plan for future lessons.

👥 STUDENT'S ROLE

- Listen actively.
- Share ideas and opinions with others.
- Make connections to other readings and to own experiences.
- Ask genuine questions and build on the ideas of others.
- Demonstrate understanding of critical literacy concepts.

Whole-group lessons lay the foundation for the day's instruction and give students the tools they will need to apply what they have learned in other contexts, including small-group instruction and independent literacy work.

PLANNING FOR COMPREHENSIVE LANGUAGE & LITERACY INSTRUCTION

For each lesson, or week of instruction, select from the menu of items shown on the Suggested Weekly Focus page, or use all of them.

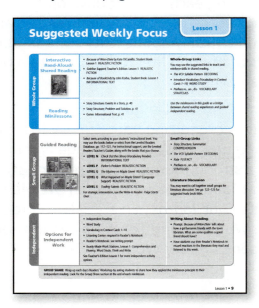

◀ Plan whole-group teaching using the menu of options provided.

WHOLE-GROUP LESSONS The Whole-Group Lessons are related lesson sequences you may want to use across a week. At the core of each lesson is a *Journeys* literature selection, chosen to highlight a certain aspect of reading that is important for students to learn and apply in various contexts.

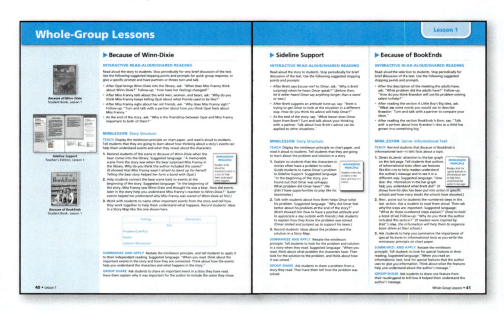

▲ Interactive Read-Aloud/Shared Reading and Reading Minilessons build and expand students' understandings, using a *Journeys* literature selection.

2 • Whole-Group Teaching

JOURNEYS RESOURCES FOR WHOLE-GROUP TEACHING
- Student Book
- Student Magazine
- Teacher's Edition Read-Alouds

Parts of Whole-Group Lessons

1 **Interactive Read-Aloud/Shared Reading** sets the stage for the day's focus and provides a common foundation of experience for students at various levels of reading proficiency (Fountas and Pinnell, 2006). In Interactive Read-Aloud/Shared Reading, you read aloud to students and encourage discussion of the reading through questions and prompts at planned stopping points in the text. Reading aloud to students in this context will help students appreciate literature, and they benefit from your modeling of how to think about ideas in the text as well as from the thinking of their peers. In addition, Interactive Read-Aloud/Shared Reading

- serves as a model of fluent, expressive, phrased reading.
- provides a context for getting students to think actively about what they read.
- allows students to hear a variety of perspectives and interpretations.
- is the common text used as an example in the Reading Minilesson.

2 The **Reading Minilesson** is the second part of your lesson. The minilesson is focused instruction about a specific topic or skill, called the Minilesson Principle (Fountas and Pinnell, 2001). Using this principle, you help your students think like effective, independent readers. The literature selection from Interactive Read-Aloud/Shared Reading context is used as the example to demonstrate the principle.

TEACHING GENRE Genre instruction is a powerful tool for helping students develop the competencies of effective readers and writers. The questions and teaching points in this section can be used over and over across the year as students encounter different genres and increasingly difficult texts within a particular genre.

▲ Integrate meaningful genre instruction into your whole-group teaching. Select from the teaching points, questions, and materials provided.

Whole-Group Teaching • 3

Small-Group Teaching

 TEACHER'S ROLE

GUIDED READING
- Form groups based on students' instructional levels.
- Establish routines and meeting times.
- Select and introduce the book.
- Monitor students' reading through the use of running records and specific questioning.
- Record observations.

LITERATURE DISCUSSION
- Form groups based on students' reading preferences.
- Demonstrate routines for effective discussion.
- Facilitate discussions, and redirect student talk as needed.
- Summarize students' ideas and engage them in self-evaluation of their contributions.

STUDENT'S ROLE

GUIDED READING
- Apply skills learned during whole-group instruction.
- Share ideas.
- Make connections to other readings and to own experiences.
- Ask questions.
- Support thinking with evidence from the text.

LITERATURE DISCUSSION
- Choose a book.
- Prepare by reading and thinking about the text.
- Listen politely and respectfully to others.
- Share opinions and raise questions.

Small-group lessons are the individualized sessions in which you help students develop as readers based on their needs, challenges, and sometimes their preferences.

GUIDED READING In guided reading lessons, you use *Journeys* Leveled Readers to work with small groups of students who will benefit from teaching at a particular instructional level. You select the text and guide the readers by supporting their ability to use a variety of reading strategies (Fountas and Pinnell, 1996, 2001). Guided reading groups are flexible and should change as a result of your observations of your students' growth.

In this guide, whole-group lessons provide the foundation for small-group instruction. Skills introduced in whole group can be developed and expanded according to students' needs in a smaller group with the appropriate level text. On the Suggested Weekly Focus pages, Leveled Readers that connect to the whole-group experience are suggested, though you may need to select from the complete Leveled Readers Database (pp. 112–121) to match your students' instructional levels.

PLANNING AND RESOURCES Using the small-group resources in this guide, along with the Leveled Readers and the Leveled Readers Teacher's Guides, you can plan for and teach lessons that will develop the competencies of your particular students. In Lessons 26–30, you have the option of using longer texts for guided reading.

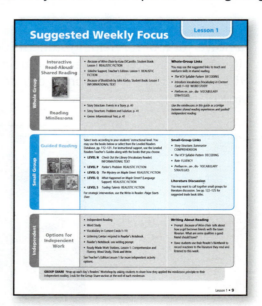

◀ Plan small-group teaching by considering the options on the Suggested Weekly Focus or in the complete Leveled Readers Database.

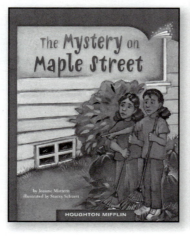
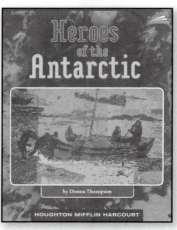

◀ **JOURNEYS Leveled Readers** Select Leveled Readers according to the instructional levels of your students.

4 • Small-Group Teaching

JOURNEYS RESOURCES FOR SMALL-GROUP TEACHING
- Leveled Readers
- Leveled Readers Teacher's Guides

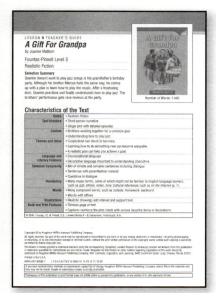
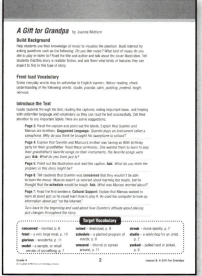
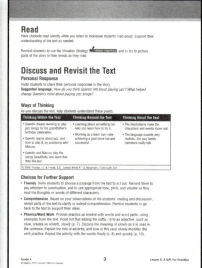
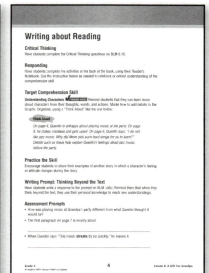

▲ **JOURNEYS Leveled Readers Teacher's Guides**

Support students as they read Leveled Readers at their instructional level. Use lessons in the Leveled Readers Teacher's Guides to promote the following:

- Thinking Within the Text
- Thinking Beyond the Text
- Thinking About the Text
- Writing About Reading
- English Language Development
- Phrased, Fluent Reading

LITERATURE DISCUSSION Literature discussion brings together a small group of students of varying abilities but who may have a common interest—a topic, a genre, or author. Students have selected the same book to read and have prepared to discuss it. In this collaborative group, you facilitate discussion of the book and encourage students to share their thinking and to build upon each other's ideas as they gain a deeper understanding of the text (Fountas and Pinnell, 2001).

The members of literature discussion groups will change as students select different titles or topics. One advantage of Literature Discussion is that all readers can benefit from each other's thinking, regardless of their instructional level.

It is important to guide students in selecting books. Introducing a range of books through book talks is one way of sharing several options for reading. Encourage students to sample a book, or read a short segment, to determine whether it is too easy or too difficult before they make a final selection. If a text choice is hard for the student to read, someone can read the text to him or her at school or at home.

A wealth of trade books can be used for engaging literature discussions. The Suggested Trade Book Titles on pp. 122–125 are appropriate for Grade 4 students, and a wide variety of genres, authors, and topics are represented. Select books from this list and make them available for students, or use books in your library.

Small-Group Teaching • 5

Independent Literacy Work

 TEACHER'S ROLE

- Establish classroom routines for independent work time.
- Set expectations for what students should accomplish.
- Confer with individual students to discuss books or sample oral reading.

STUDENT'S ROLE

- Follow established classroom routines.
- Engage thoughtfully in reading and writing tasks.
- Take responsibility for assignments, and demonstrate progress.

Independent literacy work includes meaningful and productive activities for your students to do while you work with small groups.

It is important that your students engage in meaningful, productive activities when you are working with other students (Fountas and Pinnell, 1996). This is an opportunity for your students to build mileage as readers, to develop good independent work skills, to collaborate with others, and to work at their own pace. The Suggested Weekly Focus for each lesson provides options for independent work that expand on the week's instruction.

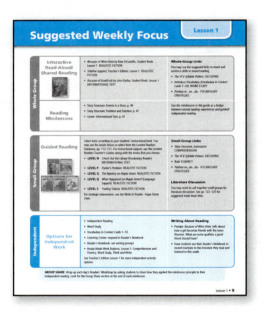

◀ Select from the options for independent work that align with instructional goals.

INDEPENDENT READING The best way to develop reading skills is to read more. Independent reading is a time for students to explore their interests, select books that are "just right" for them, and read continuous text for an established period of time. Support your students as they make book choices because too-hard books will only frustrate them. Teach them how to choose books that they can read with understanding and that don't present too many challenges. Having a large, accessible collection of books—whether in your classroom or in the library—is the best way to support readers.

6 • Independent Literacy Work

JOURNEYS RESOURCES TO SUPPORT INDEPENDENT LITERACY WORK
- Student Book Audiotext CD
- Vocabulary in Context Cards
- Ready-Made Work Stations

READER'S NOTEBOOK A Reader's Notebook is a place for students to respond to their reading and to provide evidence of their understanding. The options for what students may write are endless—letters to you, letters to authors, lists, narratives, poems, book reviews, and journal entries. You may ask them to write about something specific or leave it open for the student to choose. A suggested prompt that links to the week's reading is provided on each Suggested Weekly Focus page.

LISTENING CENTER Using a Listening Center will improve students' listening comprehension and expand their vocabulary. It is also an effective way to have students listen to models of fluent reading. Students may respond to the story or book in their Reader's Notebook.

WORD STUDY Expose students to a wide variety of meaningful word study activities. Word sorting, synonyms and antonyms, idioms, compound words, parts of speech, and word parts are just some examples of word study topics that can be developed into independent literacy activities. The Vocabulary in Context Cards for a given lesson contain words used in the week's literature. On the back of each card, a student-friendly explanation of the word and activities are provided to help students think about how the word can be used in various contexts.

▲ Vocabulary in Context Cards

READY-MADE WORK STATIONS The *Journeys* Ready-Made Work Stations link to the week's literature and skills in three strands of literacy instruction: comprehension and fluency, word study, and writing. Three different activities are provided on each card, providing students with multiple opportunities to practice the skill.

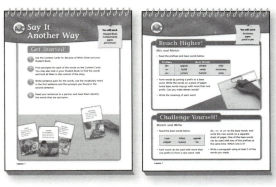

▲ Ready-Made Work Stations

Independent Literacy Work • 7

Planning for Comprehensive Language and Literacy Instruction

Effective teaching begins with careful observation of your students' literacy behaviors, systematic initial and ongoing assessment, and thoughtful planning to meet the literacy needs of your students. In this guide, you will find a consistent structure and a rich collection of resources with a menu of items and lessons to guide your teaching. You will need to tailor your teaching decisions within the lessons to fit the strengths and needs of your particular students.

On the pages that follow, you will find a Suggested Weekly Focus for each lesson. Options are included for each part of the Readers' Workshop.

- **Whole-Group Teaching:** Interactive Read-Aloud/Shared Reading, Reading Minilessons, Suggested Links for Teaching and Reinforcing Skills
- **Small-Group Teaching:** Guided Reading and Literature Discussion, Suggested Links for Teaching and Reinforcing Skills
- **Independent Work:** Independent Reading, Writing About Reading, Word Study, Ready-Made Work Stations, Vocabulary in Context Cards

Suggested Weekly Focus

Lesson 1	9	Lesson 16	24
Lesson 2	10	Lesson 17	25
Lesson 3	11	Lesson 18	26
Lesson 4	12	Lesson 19	27
Lesson 5	13	Lesson 20	28
Lesson 6	14	Lesson 21	29
Lesson 7	15	Lesson 22	30
Lesson 8	16	Lesson 23	31
Lesson 9	17	Lesson 24	32
Lesson 10	18	Lesson 25	33
Lesson 11	19	Lesson 26	34
Lesson 12	20	Lesson 27	35
Lesson 13	21	Lesson 28	36
Lesson 14	22	Lesson 29	37
Lesson 15	23	Lesson 30	38

Suggested Weekly Focus

Lesson 1

Whole Group

Interactive Read-Aloud/Shared Reading

- *Because of Winn-Dixie* by Kate DiCamillo, Student Book: Lesson 1 REALISTIC FICTION
- *Sideline Support,* Teacher's Edition: Lesson 1 REALISTIC FICTION
- *Because of BookEnds* by John Korba, Student Book: Lesson 1 INFORMATIONAL TEXT

Whole-Group Links

You may use the suggested links to teach and reinforce skills in shared reading.

- *The VCV Syllable Pattern* DECODING
- *Introduce Vocabulary (Vocabulary in Context Cards 1–10)* WORD STUDY
- *Prefixes* re-, un-, dis- VOCABULARY STRATEGIES

Use the minilessons in this guide as a bridge between shared reading experiences and guided/independent reading.

Reading Minilessons

- Story Structure: Events in a Story, p. 40
- Story Structure: Problem and Solution, p. 41
- Genre: Informational Text, p. 41

Small Group

Guided Reading

Select texts according to your students' instructional level. You may use the books below or select from the Leveled Readers Database, pp. 112–121. For instructional support, use the Leveled Readers Teacher's Guides along with the books that you choose.

- **LEVEL N** *Check Out the Library* (Vocabulary Reader) INFORMATIONAL TEXT
- **LEVEL P** *Parker's Problem* REALISTIC FICTION
- **LEVEL Q** *The Mystery on Maple Street* REALISTIC FICTION
- **LEVEL Q** *What Happened on Maple Street?* (Language Support) REALISTIC FICTION
- **LEVEL S** *Trading Talents* REALISTIC FICTION

For strategic intervention, use the Write-In Reader: *Paige Starts Over.*

Small-Group Links

- *Story Structure; Summarize* COMPREHENSION
- *The VCV Syllable Pattern* DECODING
- *Rate* FLUENCY
- *Prefixes* re-, un-, dis- VOCABULARY STRATEGIES

Literature Discussion

You may want to call together small groups for literature discussion. See pp. 122–125 for suggested trade book titles.

Independent

Options for Independent Work

- Independent Reading
- Word Study
- Vocabulary in Context Cards 1–10
- Listening Center: respond in Reader's Notebook
- Reader's Notebook: see writing prompt
- Ready-Made Work Stations, Lesson 1: Comprehension and Fluency, Word Study, Think and Write

See Teacher's Edition Lesson 1 for more independent activity options.

Writing About Reading

- Prompt: *Because of Winn-Dixie* tells about how a girl becomes friends with the town librarian. What are some qualities a good friend should have?
- Have students use their Reader's Notebook to record reactions to the literature they read and listened to this week.

GROUP SHARE Wrap up each day's Readers' Workshop by asking students to share how they applied the minilesson principle to their independent reading. Look for the Group Share section at the end of each minilesson.

Suggested Weekly Focus

Lesson 2

Whole Group

Interactive Read-Aloud/Shared Reading

- *My Brother Martin: A Sister Remembers Growing Up with the Rev. Dr. Martin Luther King, Jr.* by Christine King Farris, Student Book: Lesson 2 BIOGRAPHY
- *The Troublemaker Who Healed a Nation,* Teacher's Edition: Lesson 2 BIOGRAPHY
- *Langston Hughes: A Poet and a Dreamer,* Student Book: Lesson 2 POETRY

Whole-Group Links

You may use the suggested links to teach and reinforce skills in shared reading.

- *Open and Closed Syllables* DECODING
- *Introduce Vocabulary* (Vocabulary in Context Cards 11–20) WORD STUDY
- *Prefixes* in-, im-, il-, ir- VOCABULARY STRATEGIES

Reading Minilessons

- Genre: Biography, p. 42
- Author's Purpose: Using Genre to Explain It, p. 43
- Genre: Poetry, p. 43

Use the minilessons in this guide as a bridge between shared reading experiences and guided/independent reading.

Small Group

Guided Reading

Select texts according to your students' instructional level. You may use the books below or select from the Leveled Readers Database, pp. 112–121. For instructional support, use the Leveled Readers Teacher's Guides along with the books that you choose.

- **LEVEL O** *Sharing a Dream* BIOGRAPHY
- **LEVEL Q** *Separate Worlds* (Vocabulary Reader) INFORMATIONAL TEXT
- **LEVEL S** *Thurgood Marshall* (Language Support) BIOGRAPHY
- **LEVEL S** *A Voice for Equality* BIOGRAPHY
- **LEVEL U** *A Leader for All* BIOGRAPHY

For strategic intervention, use the Write-In Reader: *Gwendolyn Brooks.*

Small-Group Links

- *Author's Purpose; Monitor/Clarify* COMPREHENSION
- *Open and Closed Syllables* DECODING
- *Phrasing: Pauses* FLUENCY
- *Prefixes* in-, im-, il-, ir- VOCABULARY STRATEGIES

Literature Discussion

You may want to call together small groups for literature discussion. See pp. 122–125 for suggested trade book titles.

Independent

Options for Independent Work

- Independent Reading
- Word Study
- Vocabulary in Context Cards 11–20
- Listening Center: respond in Reader's Notebook
- Reader's Notebook: see writing prompt
- Ready-Made Work Stations, Lesson 2: Comprehension and Fluency, Word Study, Think and Write

See Teacher's Edition Lesson 2 for more independent activity options.

Writing About Reading

- Prompt: *The Troublemaker Who Healed a Nation* is a biography of Nelson Mandela. Write a short biography of a person that you respect.
- Have students use their Reader's Notebook to record reactions to the literature they read and listened to this week.

GROUP SHARE Wrap up each day's Readers' Workshop by asking students to share how they applied the minilesson principle to their independent reading. Look for the Group Share section at the end of each minilesson.

Suggested Weekly Focus

Lesson 3

Whole Group

Interactive Read-Aloud/ Shared Reading

- *How Tía Lola Came to Stay* by Julia Alvarez, Student Book: Lesson 3 REALISTIC FICTION
- *Hannah in California,* Teacher's Edition: Lesson 3 REALISTIC FICTION
- *Pizza Pizzazz* by Peter Sylvia, Student Book: Lesson 3 INFORMATIONAL TEXT

Whole-Group Links

You may use the suggested links to teach and reinforce skills in shared reading.

- *The VCCV Syllable Pattern* DECODING
- *Introduce Vocabulary (Vocabulary in Context Cards 21–30)* WORD STUDY
- *Context Clues* VOCABULARY STRATEGIES

Reading Minilessons

- Cause and Effect: Understanding Events, p. 44
- Cause and Effect: How Events Affect Characters, p. 45
- Directions: How Authors Explain a Process, p. 45

Use the minilessons in this guide as a bridge between shared reading experiences and guided/independent reading.

Small Group

Guided Reading

Select texts according to your students' instructional level. You may use the books below or select from the Leveled Readers Database, pp. 112–121. For instructional support, use the Leveled Readers Teacher's Guides along with the books that you choose.

- **LEVEL N** *New Kid on the Court* REALISTIC FICTION
- **LEVEL N** *A Visit to the Dominican Republic* (Vocabulary Reader) INFORMATIONAL TEXT
- **LEVEL R** *I Will Not Eat That!* (Language Support) REALISTIC FICTION
- **LEVEL R** *The Picky Eater* REALISTIC FICTION
- **LEVEL T** *My Sister's Surprise* REALISTIC FICTION

For strategic intervention, use the Write-In Reader: *The Flan Plan.*

Small-Group Links

- *Cause and Effect; Visualize* COMPREHENSION
- *The VCCV Syllable Pattern* DECODING
- *Accuracy* FLUENCY
- *Context Clues* VOCABULARY STRATEGIES

Literature Discussion

You may want to call together small groups for literature discussion. See pp. 122–125 for suggested trade book titles.

Independent

Options for Independent Work

- Independent Reading
- Word Study
- Vocabulary in Context Cards 21–30
- Listening Center: respond in Reader's Notebook
- Reader's Notebook: see writing prompt
- Ready-Made Work Stations, Lesson 3: Comprehension and Fluency, Word Study, Think and Write

See Teacher's Edition Lesson 3 for more independent activity options.

Writing About Reading

- Prompt: *Pizza Pizzazz* tells you how to design your own pizza. Write an advertisement for the pizza that you would make. Tell what the name is and why you think others will like it.
- Have students use their Reader's Notebook to record reactions to the literature they read and listened to this week.

GROUP SHARE Wrap up each day's Readers' Workshop by asking students to share how they applied the minilesson principle to their independent reading. Look for the Group Share section at the end of each minilesson.

Suggested Weekly Focus

Lesson 4

Whole Group

Interactive Read-Aloud/Shared Reading

- *The Power of W.O.W.!* by Crystal Hubbard, Student Book: Lesson 4 PLAY
- *Bookmobile Rescue,* Teacher's Edition: Lesson 4 REALISTIC FICTION
- *Knowing Noses: Search-and-Rescue Dogs* by Ellen Gold, Student Book: Lesson 4 INFORMATIONAL TEXT

Whole-Group Links

You may use the suggested links to teach and reinforce skills in shared reading.

- *VCV and VCCV Syllable Patterns* DECODING
- *Introduce Vocabulary (Vocabulary in Context Cards 31–40)* WORD STUDY
- *Prefixes* non-, mis- VOCABULARY STRATEGIES

Reading Minilessons

- Theme: Understanding Characters' Actions, p. 46
- Genre: Realistic Fiction, p. 47
- Genre: Informational Text, p. 47

Use the minilessons in this guide as a bridge between shared reading experiences and guided/independent reading.

Small Group

Guided Reading

Select texts according to your students' instructional level. You may use the books below or select from the Leveled Readers Database, pp. 112–121. For instructional support, use the Leveled Readers Teacher's Guides along with the books that you choose.

- **LEVEL N** *Nina Wows KWOW* PLAY
- **LEVEL O** *Community Teamwork* (Vocabulary Reader) INFORMATIONAL TEXT
- **LEVEL O** *Friends on a Field Trip* (Language Support) PLAY
- **LEVEL P** *A Friendly Field Trip* PLAY
- **LEVEL S** *A.L.L. to the Rescue* PLAY

For strategic intervention, use the Write-In Reader: *Concert for a Cause.*

Small-Group Links

- *Theme; Analyze/Evaluate* COMPREHENSION
- *VCV and VCCV Syllable Patterns* DECODING
- *Intonation* FLUENCY
- *Prefixes* non-, mis- VOCABULARY STRATEGIES

Literature Discussion

You may want to call together small groups for literature discussion. See pp. 122–125 for suggested trade book titles.

Independent

Options for Independent Work

- Independent Reading
- Word Study
- Vocabulary in Context Cards 31–40
- Listening Center: respond in Reader's Notebook
- Reader's Notebook: see writing prompt
- Ready-Made Work Stations, Lesson 4: Comprehension and Fluency, Word Study, Think and Write

See Teacher's Edition Lesson 4 for more independent activity options.

Writing About Reading

- **Prompt:** *The Power of W.O.W.!* is about children who figure out how to save a bookmobile. Write a short thank-you note from the librarian to the children who helped save the bookmobile.
- Have students use their Reader's Notebook to record reactions to the literature they read and listened to this week.

GROUP SHARE Wrap up each day's Readers' Workshop by asking students to share how they applied the minilesson principle to their independent reading. Look for the Group Share section at the end of each minilesson.

Suggested Weekly Focus

Lesson 5

Whole Group

Interactive Read-Aloud/ Shared Reading

- *Stormalong* by Mary Pope Osborne, Student Book: Lesson 5 TALL TALE
- *Mighty Joe Magarac,* Teacher's Edition: Lesson 5 TALL TALE
- *Hoderi the Fisherman* retold by Kate McGovern, Student Book: Lesson 5 PLAY/FOLKTALE

Whole-Group Links

You may use the suggested links to teach and reinforce skills in shared reading.

- *Homophones* DECODING
- *Introduce Vocabulary* (Vocabulary in Context Cards 41–50) WORD STUDY
- *Use a Dictionary* VOCABULARY STRATEGIES

Reading Minilessons

- Understanding Characters: Main Characters, p. 48
- Understanding Characters: Making Predictions, p. 49
- Genre: Play, p. 49

Use the minilessons in this guide as a bridge between shared reading experiences and guided/independent reading.

Small Group

Guided Reading

Select texts according to your students' instructional level. You may use the books below or select from the Leveled Readers Database, pp. 112–121. For instructional support, use the Leveled Readers Teacher's Guides along with the books that you choose.

- **LEVEL P** *Mississippi Marvis Barnes* TALL TALE
- **LEVEL P** *The Golden Age of Sail* (Vocabulary Reader) INFORMATIONAL TEXT
- **LEVEL P** *The Amazing Balina* (Language Support) TALL TALE
- **LEVEL Q** *Balina* TALL TALE
- **LEVEL R** *Whisper* TALL TALE

For strategic intervention, use the Write-In Reader: *Babe's Vacation.*

Small-Group Links

- *Understanding Characters; Infer/Predict* COMPREHENSION
- *Homophones* DECODING
- *Expression* FLUENCY
- *Use a Dictionary* VOCABULARY STRATEGIES

Literature Discussion

You may want to call together small groups for literature discussion. See pp. 122–125 for suggested trade book titles.

Independent

Options for Independent Work

- Independent Reading
- Word Study
- Vocabulary in Context Cards 41–50
- Listening Center: respond in Reader's Notebook
- Reader's Notebook: see writing prompt
- Ready-Made Work Stations, Lesson 5: Comprehension and Fluency, Word Study, Think and Write

See Teacher's Edition Lesson 5 for more independent activity options.

Writing About Reading

- Prompt: The author of *Stormalong* describes things that are larger than life. Explain which descriptions best caught your attention as a reader, and tell why.
- Have students use their Reader's Notebook to record reactions to the literature they read and listened to this week.

GROUP SHARE Wrap up each day's Readers' Workshop by asking students to share how they applied the minilesson principle to their independent reading. Look for the Group Share section at the end of each minilesson.

Lesson 5 • 13

Suggested Weekly Focus

Lesson 6

Whole Group

Interactive Read-Aloud/Shared Reading

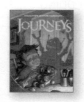

- *Once Upon a Cool Motorcycle Dude* by Kevin O'Malley, Student Book: Lesson 6 FAIRY TALE
- *Tim Wishes Twice,* Teacher's Edition: Lesson 6 FANTASY
- *Storyteller Diane Ferlatte* by Ellen Gold, Student Book: Lesson 6 INFORMATIONAL TEXT

Whole-Group Links

You may use the suggested links to teach and reinforce skills in shared reading.

- *Common Consonant Patterns: Digraphs* DECODING
- *Introduce Vocabulary (Vocabulary in Context Cards 51–60)* WORD STUDY
- *Suffixes -y, -ous* VOCABULARY STRATEGIES

Reading Minilessons

- Compare and Contrast: How Characters Are Alike and Different, p. 50
- Understanding Characters: Characters' Choices, p. 51
- Genre: Informational Text, p. 51

Use the minilessons in this guide as a bridge between shared reading experiences and guided/independent reading.

Small Group

Guided Reading

Select texts according to your students' instructional level. You may use the books below or select from the Leveled Readers Database, pp. 112–121. For instructional support, use the Leveled Readers Teacher's Guides along with the books that you choose.

- **LEVEL M** *Ike in the Spotlight* FAIRY TALE
- **LEVEL Q** *Storytelling Through the Years* (Vocabulary Reader) INFORMATIONAL TEXT
- **LEVEL S** *Rosa's Adventure* (Language Support) FAIRY TALE
- **LEVEL S** *A Pen and a Painting* FAIRY TALE
- **LEVEL T** *The Lark Sings in Many Colors* FAIRY TALE

For strategic intervention, use the Write-In Reader: *The Three Little Pigs Go Online.*

Small-Group Links

- *Compare and Contrast; Infer/Predict* COMPREHENSION
- *Common Consonant Patterns: Digraphs* DECODING
- *Expression* FLUENCY
- *Suffixes -y, -ous* VOCABULARY STRATEGIES

Literature Discussion

You may want to call together small groups for literature discussion. See pp. 122–125 for suggested trade book titles.

Independent

Options for Independent Work

- Independent Reading
- Word Study
- Vocabulary in Context Cards 51–60
- Listening Center: respond in Reader's Notebook
- Reader's Notebook: see writing prompt
- Ready-Made Work Stations, Lesson 6: Comprehension and Fluency, Word Study, Think and Write

See Teacher's Edition Lesson 6 for more independent activity options.

Writing About Reading

- Prompt: *Once Upon a Cool Motorcycle Dude* is a new kind of fairy tale. Think about another fairy tale you know. How are the two fairy tales alike and how are they different?
- Have students use their Reader's Notebook to record reactions to the literature they read and listened to this week.

GROUP SHARE Wrap up each day's Readers' Workshop by asking students to share how they applied the minilesson principle to their independent reading. Look for the Group Share section at the end of each minilesson.

Suggested Weekly Focus

Lesson 7

Whole Group

Interactive Read-Aloud/Shared Reading

- *Coming Distractions: Questioning Movies* by Frank W. Baker, Student Book: Lesson 7 INFORMATIONAL TEXT
- *Steven Spielberg: A Filmmaker's Journey,* Teacher's Edition: Lesson 7 INFORMATIONAL TEXT
- *The Wonder of Animation* by Grace V. Montek, Student Book: Lesson 7 INFORMATIONAL TEXT

Whole-Group Links

You may use the suggested links to teach and reinforce skills in shared reading.

- *Common Consonant Patterns: Clusters* DECODING
- *Introduce Vocabulary (Vocabulary in Context Cards 61–70)* WORD STUDY
- *Greek and Latin Word Parts* phon, photo, graph, auto VOCABULARY STRATEGIES

Reading Minilessons

- Fact and Opinion: Difference Between Facts and Opinions, p. 52
- Fact and Opinion: Recognizing Differences, p. 53
- Genre: Informational Text, p. 53

Use the minilessons in this guide as a bridge between shared reading experiences and guided/independent reading.

Small Group

Guided Reading

Select texts according to your students' instructional level. You may use the books below or select from the Leveled Readers Database, pp. 112–121. For instructional support, use the Leveled Readers Teacher's Guides along with the books that you choose.

- **LEVEL P** *Now Showing in Your Living Room* INFORMATIONAL TEXT
- **LEVEL P** *Behind the Scenes* (Vocabulary Reader) INFORMATIONAL TEXT
- **LEVEL T** *Making Movies* (Language Support) INFORMATIONAL TEXT
- **LEVEL T** *The Magic of Movies* INFORMATIONAL TEXT
- **LEVEL V** *Critics in Hollywood* INFORMATIONAL TEXT

For strategic intervention, use the Write-In Reader: *Film Facts.*

Small-Group Links

- *Fact and Opinion; Summarize* COMPREHENSION
- *Common Consonant Patterns: Clusters* DECODING
- *Phrasing: Punctuation* FLUENCY
- *Greek and Latin Word Parts* phon, photo, graph, auto VOCABULARY STRATEGIES

Literature Discussion

You may want to call together small groups for literature discussion. See pp. 122–125 for suggested trade book titles.

Independent

Options for Independent Work

- Independent Reading
- Word Study
- Vocabulary in Context Cards 61–70
- Listening Center: respond in Reader's Notebook
- Reader's Notebook: see writing prompt
- Ready-Made Work Stations, Lesson 7: Comprehension and Fluency, Word Study, Think and Write

See Teacher's Edition Lesson 7 for more independent activity options.

Writing About Reading

- Prompt: The author of *Steven Spielberg: A Filmmaker's Journey* tells about the life of a famous filmmaker. Would you want to make films? Tell why or why not.
- Have students use their Reader's Notebook to record reactions to the literature they read and listened to this week.

GROUP SHARE Wrap up each day's Readers' Workshop by asking students to share how they applied the minilesson principle to their independent reading. Look for the Group Share section at the end of each minilesson.

Suggested Weekly Focus

Lesson 8

Whole Group

Interactive Read-Aloud/ Shared Reading

- *Me and Uncle Romie* by Claire Hartfield, Student Book: Lesson 8 REALISTIC FICTION
- *Jazzy Jasmine,* Teacher's Edition: Lesson 8 REALISTIC FICTION
- *Sidewalk Artists* by Sam Rabe, Student Book: Lesson 8 READERS' THEATER

Whole-Group Links

You may use the suggested links to teach and reinforce skills in shared reading.

- *Stressed and Unstressed Syllables* DECODING
- *Introduce Vocabulary (Vocabulary in Context Cards 71–80)* WORD STUDY
- *Figurative Language (Idioms)* VOCABULARY STRATEGIES

Reading Minilessons

- Understanding Characters: Getting to Know Characters, p. 54
- Understanding Characters: How Characters Influence One Another, p. 55
- Directions: Steps in a Process, p. 55

Use the minilessons in this guide as a bridge between shared reading experiences and guided/ independent reading.

Small Group

Guided Reading

Select texts according to your students' instructional level. You may use the books below or select from the Leveled Readers Database, pp. 112–121. For instructional support, use the Leveled Readers Teacher's Guides along with the books that you choose.

- **LEVEL M** *Recipe for Learning* REALISTIC FICTION
- **LEVEL R** *Romare Bearden* (Vocabulary Reader) INFORMATIONAL TEXT
- **LEVEL S** *A Gift for Grandpa* (Language Support) REALISTIC FICTION
- **LEVEL S** *Gramp's Favorite Gift* REALISTIC FICTION
- **LEVEL S** *Stuck at Camp* REALISTIC FICTION

For strategic intervention, use the Write-In Reader: *Summer in the City.*

Small-Group Links

- *Understanding Characters; Visualize* COMPREHENSION
- *Stressed and Unstressed Syllables* DECODING
- *Stress* FLUENCY
- *Figurative Language (Idioms)* VOCABULARY STRATEGIES

Literature Discussion

You may want to call together small groups for literature discussion. See pp. 122–125 for suggested trade book titles.

Independent

Options for Independent Work

- Independent Reading
- Word Study
- Vocabulary in Context Cards 71–80
- Listening Center: respond in Reader's Notebook
- Reader's Notebook: see writing prompt
- Ready-Made Work Stations, Lesson 8: Comprehension and Fluency, Word Study, Think and Write

See Teacher's Edition Lesson 8 for more independent activity options.

Writing About Reading

- Prompt: *Sidewalk Artists* is a play that tells about children who make chalk drawings outside. Think of a chalk drawing you would like to make. Describe it with vivid language.
- Have students use their Reader's Notebook to record reactions to the literature they read and listened to this week.

GROUP SHARE Wrap up each day's Readers' Workshop by asking students to share how they applied the minilesson principle to their independent reading. Look for the Group Share section at the end of each minilesson.

Suggested Weekly Focus

Lesson 9

Whole Group

Interactive Read-Aloud/Shared Reading

- *Dear Mr. Winston* by Ken Roberts, Student Book: Lesson 9 REALISTIC FICTION
- *Is Sasquatch Out There?* Teacher's Edition: Lesson 9 INFORMATIONAL TEXT
- *Field Guide to Snakes of the Southwest* by Patrick Sutter, Student Book: Lesson 9 INFORMATIONAL TEXT

Whole-Group Links

You may use the suggested links to teach and reinforce skills in shared reading.

- *Common Beginning Syllables* DECODING
- *Introduce Vocabulary (Vocabulary in Context Cards 81–90)* WORD STUDY
- *Antonyms* VOCABULARY STRATEGIES

Reading Minilessons

- Conclusions: Using Clues to Draw Conclusions, p. 56
- Conclusions: Forming Opinions, p. 57
- Genre: Informational Text, p. 57

Use the minilessons in this guide as a bridge between shared reading experiences and guided/independent reading.

Small Group

Guided Reading

Select texts according to your students' instructional level. You may use the books below or select from the Leveled Readers Database, pp. 112–121. For instructional support, use the Leveled Readers Teacher's Guides along with the books that you choose.

- **LEVEL M** *Painting the Ocean* REALISTIC FICTION
- **LEVEL O** *Reptiles As Pets* (Vocabulary Reader) INFORMATIONAL TEXT
- **LEVEL R** *Sisters Play Soccer* (Language Support) REALISTIC FICTION
- **LEVEL R** *Soccer Sisters* REALISTIC FICTION
- **LEVEL S** *Think Before You Speak* REALISTIC FICTION

For strategic intervention, use the Write-In Reader: *Snake Hunt*.

Small-Group Links

- *Conclusions and Generalizations; Question* COMPREHENSION
- *Common Beginning Syllables* DECODING
- *Accuracy* FLUENCY
- *Antonyms* VOCABULARY STRATEGIES

Literature Discussion

You may want to call together small groups for literature discussion. See pp. 122–125 for suggested trade book titles.

Independent

Options for Independent Work

- Independent Reading
- Word Study
- Vocabulary in Context Cards 81–90
- Listening Center: respond in Reader's Notebook
- Reader's Notebook: see writing prompt
- Ready-Made Work Stations, Lesson 9: Comprehension and Fluency, Word Study, Think and Write

See Teacher's Edition Lesson 9 for more independent activity options.

Writing About Reading

- Prompt: *Dear Mr. Winston* is a letter that a girl writes to a librarian she scared with a snake. What might Mr. Winston say to the girl after reading her letter? Write what you think his response would be in a letter.
- Have students use their Reader's Notebook to record reactions to the literature they read and listened to this week.

GROUP SHARE Wrap up each day's Readers' Workshop by asking students to share how they applied the minilesson principle to their independent reading. Look for the Group Share section at the end of each minilesson.

Lesson 9 • **17**

Suggested Weekly Focus

Lesson 10

Whole Group

Interactive Read-Aloud/Shared Reading

- *José! Born to Dance* by Susanna Reich, Student Book: Lesson 10 BIOGRAPHY
- *Mexican Dove,* Teacher's Edition: Lesson 10 BIOGRAPHY
- *Dance to the Beat* by Adam Fogelberg, Student Book: Lesson 10 POETRY

Whole-Group Links

You may use the suggested links to teach and reinforce skills in shared reading.

- *Vowel + r Sound in Multi-Syllable Words* DECODING
- *Introduce Vocabulary (Vocabulary in Context Cards 91–100)* WORD STUDY
- *Analogies* VOCABULARY STRATEGIES

Reading Minilessons

- Genre: Biography, p. 58
- Author's Purpose: Author's Feelings About a Subject, p. 59
- Genre: Poetry, p. 59

Use the minilessons in this guide as a bridge between shared reading experiences and guided/independent reading.

Small Group

Guided Reading

Select texts according to your students' instructional level. You may use the books below or select from the Leveled Readers Database, pp. 112–121. For instructional support, use the Leveled Readers Teacher's Guides along with the books that you choose.

- **LEVEL O** *Isadora Duncan* BIOGRAPHY
- **LEVEL P** *Artists in Training* (Vocabulary Reader) INFORMATIONAL TEXT
- **LEVEL S** *The Life of Jackson Pollock* (Language Support) BIOGRAPHY
- **LEVEL S** *Jackson Pollock in Action* BIOGRAPHY
- **LEVEL W** *Luciano Pavarotti* BIOGRAPHY

For strategic intervention, use the Write-In Reader: *Maria Tallchief: A Life of Dance.*

Small-Group Links

- *Author's Purpose; Analyze/Evaluate* COMPREHENSION
- *Vowel + r Sound in Multi-Syllable Words* DECODING
- *Intonation* FLUENCY
- *Analogies* VOCABULARY STRATEGIES

Literature Discussion

You may want to call together small groups for literature discussion. See pp. 122–125 for suggested trade book titles.

Independent

Options for Independent Work

- Independent Reading
- Word Study
- Vocabulary in Context Cards 91–100
- Listening Center: respond in Reader's Notebook
- Reader's Notebook: see writing prompt
- Ready-Made Work Stations, Lesson 10: Comprehension and Fluency, Word Study, Think and Write

See Teacher's Edition Lesson 10 for more independent activity options.

Writing About Reading

- Prompt: *Dance to the Beat* includes a number of poems about dance. Choose one of the poems. Write a paragraph that describes what the poem makes you see and feel.
- Have students use their Reader's Notebook to record reactions to the literature they read and listened to this week.

GROUP SHARE Wrap up each day's Readers' Workshop by asking students to share how they applied the minilesson principle to their independent reading. Look for the Group Share section at the end of each minilesson.

Suggested Weekly Focus

Lesson 11

Whole Group

Interactive Read-Aloud/ Shared Reading

- *The Screech Owl Who Liked Television* by Jean Craighead George, Student Book: Lesson 11   NARRATIVE NONFICTION
- *Frisky Whiskers,* Teacher's Edition: Lesson 11 INFORMATIONAL TEXT
- *In the Wild* by Anne Patterson, Student Book: Lesson 11 READERS' THEATER

Whole-Group Links

You may use the suggested links to teach and reinforce skills in shared reading.

- *Compound Words* DECODING
- *Introduce Vocabulary (Vocabulary in Context Cards 101–110)* WORD STUDY
- *Suffixes* -ful, -less, -ness, -ment VOCABULARY STRATEGIES

Use the minilessons in this guide as a bridge between shared reading experiences and guided/ independent reading.

Reading Minilessons

- Genre: Narrative Nonfiction, p. 60
- Fact and Opinion: Supporting Opinions with Facts, p. 61
- Persuasion: How Authors Persuade, p. 61

Small Group

Guided Reading

Select texts according to your students' instructional level. You may use the books below or select from the Leveled Readers Database, pp. 112–121. For instructional support, use the Leveled Readers Teacher's Guides along with the books that you choose.

- **LEVEL O**   *Koko Communicates* NARRATIVE NONFICTION
- **LEVEL Q**   *Feathered Hunters of the Night* (Vocabulary Reader) INFORMATIONAL TEXT
- **LEVEL R**   *Inside the Zoo* (Language Support) NARRATIVE NONFICTION
- **LEVEL R**   *Going Wild at the Zoo* NARRATIVE NONFICTION
- **LEVEL S**   *An Inside Look at Zoos* NARRATIVE NONFICTION

For strategic intervention, use the Write-In Reader: *A Hike in the Park.*

Small-Group Links

- *Fact and Opinion; Infer/Predict* COMPREHENSION
- *Compound Words* DECODING
- *Phrasing: Punctuation* FLUENCY
- *Suffixes* -ful, -less, -ness, -ment VOCABULARY STRATEGIES

Literature Discussion

You may want to call together small groups for literature discussion. See pp. 122–125 for suggested trade book titles.

Independent

Options for Independent Work

- Independent Reading
- Word Study
- Vocabulary in Context Cards 101–110
- Listening Center: respond in Reader's Notebook
- Reader's Notebook: see writing prompt
- Ready-Made Work Stations, Lesson 11: Comprehension and Fluency, Word Study, Think and Write

See Teacher's Edition Lesson 11 for more independent activity options.

Writing About Reading

- Prompt: *The Screech Owl Who Liked Television* is a story about a pet owl that a family raises. Do you think people should keep wild animals as pets? Why or why not?
- Have students use their Reader's Notebook to record reactions to the literature they read and listened to this week.

GROUP SHARE Wrap up each day's Readers' Workshop by asking students to share how they applied the minilesson principle to their independent reading. Look for the Group Share section at the end of each minilesson.

Suggested Weekly Focus

Lesson 12

Whole Group

Interactive Read-Aloud/Shared Reading

- *The Earth Dragon Awakes* by Laurence Yep, Student Book: Lesson 12   HISTORICAL FICTION
- *Safe from Harm*, Teacher's Edition: Lesson 12   REALISTIC FICTION
- *Texas Twisters*, Student Book: Lesson 12   INFORMATIONAL TEXT

Whole-Group Links

You may use the suggested links to teach and reinforce skills in shared reading.

- *Base Words and Endings*   DECODING
- *Introduce Vocabulary (Vocabulary in Context Cards 111–120)*   WORD STUDY
- *Synonyms*   VOCABULARY STRATEGIES

Reading Minilessons

- Sequence of Events: Using Dates and Clues, p. 62
- Sequence of Events: Understanding Passage of Time, p. 63
- Genre: Informational Text, p. 63

Use the minilessons in this guide as a bridge between shared reading experiences and guided/independent reading.

Small Group

Guided Reading

Select texts according to your students' instructional level. You may use the books below or select from the Leveled Readers Database, pp. 112–121. For instructional support, use the Leveled Readers Teacher's Guides along with the books that you choose.

- **LEVEL N**   *Sailing to Safety*   HISTORICAL FICTION
- **LEVEL O**   *Keeping Safe in an Earthquake* (Vocabulary Reader)   INFORMATIONAL TEXT
- **LEVEL R**   *A New Name for Lois* (Language Support)   HISTORICAL FICTION
- **LEVEL S**   *Little Hare and the Thundering Earth*   HISTORICAL FICTION
- **LEVEL T**   *Two Against the Mississippi*   HISTORICAL FICTION

For strategic intervention, use the Write-In Reader: *Earth on the Move*.

Small-Group Links

- *Sequence of Events; Visualize*   COMPREHENSION
- *Base Words and Endings*   DECODING
- *Adjust Rate to Purpose*   FLUENCY
- *Synonyms*   VOCABULARY STRATEGIES

Literature Discussion

You may want to call together small groups for literature discussion. See pp. 122–125 for suggested trade book titles.

Independent

Options for Independent Work

- Independent Reading
- Word Study
- Vocabulary in Context Cards 111–120
- Listening Center: respond in Reader's Notebook
- Reader's Notebook: see writing prompt
- Ready-Made Work Stations, Lesson 12: Comprehension and Fluency, Word Study, Think and Write

See Teacher's Edition Lesson 12 for more independent activity options.

Writing About Reading

- Prompt: *The Earth Dragon Awakes* and *Safe from Harm* both tell about the destruction nature can cause. Write a paragraph comparing an earthquake with a mudslide.
- Have students use their Reader's Notebook to record reactions to the literature they read and listened to this week.

GROUP SHARE   Wrap up each day's Readers' Workshop by asking students to share how they applied the minilesson principle to their independent reading. Look for the Group Share section at the end of each minilesson.

Suggested Weekly Focus

Lesson 13

Whole Group

Interactive Read-Aloud/Shared Reading

- *Antarctic Journal: Four Months at the Bottom of the World* by Jennifer Owings Dewey, Student Book: Lesson 13 NARRATIVE NONFICTION
- *On My Way to Meet the Khan: Excerpts from Marco Polo's Adventures,* Teacher's Edition: Lesson 13 INFORMATIONAL TEXT
- *The Coolest Marathon!* by Misha Herenger, Student Book: Lesson 13 INFORMATIONAL TEXT

Whole-Group Links

You may use the suggested links to teach and reinforce skills in shared reading.

- *Recognizing Common Word Parts* DECODING
- *Introduce Vocabulary (Vocabulary in Context Cards 121–130)* WORD STUDY
- *Greek and Latin Word Parts* spect, struct, tele, vis VOCABULARY STRATEGIES

Reading Minilessons

- Cause and Effect: Recognizing Cause, p. 64
- Cause and Effect: Recognizing Effect, p. 65
- Genre: Informational Text, p. 65

Use the minilessons in this guide as a bridge between shared reading experiences and guided/independent reading.

Small Group

Guided Reading

Select texts according to your students' instructional level. You may use the books below or select from the Leveled Readers Database, pp. 112–121. For instructional support, use the Leveled Readers Teacher's Guides along with the books that you choose.

- **LEVEL O** *Amazing Birds of Antarctica* NARRATIVE NONFICTION
- **LEVEL O** *Really, Really Cold!* (Vocabulary Reader) INFORMATIONAL TEXT
- **LEVEL R** *A Visit to Antarctica* (Language Support) NARRATIVE NONFICTION
- **LEVEL R** *An Icy Adventure* NARRATIVE NONFICTION
- **LEVEL V** *Heroes of the Antarctic* NARRATIVE NONFICTION

For strategic intervention, use the Write-In Reader: *In the Grip of Ice.*

Small-Group Links

- *Cause and Effect; Summarize* COMPREHENSION
- *Recognizing Common Word Parts* DECODING
- *Phrasing: Pauses* FLUENCY
- *Greek and Latin Word Parts* spect, struct, tele, vis VOCABULARY STRATEGIES

Literature Discussion

You may want to call together small groups for literature discussion. See pp. 122–125 for suggested trade book titles.

Independent

Options for Independent Work

- Independent Reading
- Word Study
- Vocabulary in Context Cards 121–130
- Listening Center: respond in Reader's Notebook
- Reader's Notebook: see writing prompt
- Ready-Made Work Stations, Lesson 13: Comprehension and Fluency, Word Study, Think and Write

See Teacher's Edition Lesson 13 for more independent activity options.

Writing About Reading

- Prompt: *The Coolest Marathon!* tells about a race in Antarctica. What kind of person would run in a race in such a difficult place? What are some of the person's character traits?
- Have students use their Reader's Notebook to record reactions to the literature they read and listened to this week.

GROUP SHARE Wrap up each day's Readers' Workshop by asking students to share how they applied the minilesson principle to their independent reading. Look for the Group Share section at the end of each minilesson.

Suggested Weekly Focus

Lesson 14

Whole Group

Interactive Read-Aloud/ Shared Reading

- *The Life and Times of the Ant* by Charles Micucci, Student Book: Lesson 14 INFORMATIONAL TEXT
- *Wicked Wind,* Teacher's Edition: Lesson 14 INFORMATIONAL TEXT
- *The Dove and the Ant* retold by Anne O'Brien, Student Book: Lesson 14 FABLE

Whole-Group Links

You may use the suggested links to teach and reinforce skills in shared reading.

- *Recognizing Suffixes* DECODING
- *Introduce Vocabulary (Vocabulary in Context Cards 131–140)* WORD STUDY
- *Suffixes -able, -ible* VOCABULARY STRATEGIES

Reading Minilessons

- Text and Graphic Features: Using Features to Understand Topics, p. 66
- Genre: Informational Text, p. 67
- Genre: Fable, p. 67

Use the minilessons in this guide as a bridge between shared reading experiences and guided/ independent reading.

Small Group

Guided Reading

Select texts according to your students' instructional level. You may use the books below or select from the Leveled Readers Database, pp. 112–121. For instructional support, use the Leveled Readers Teacher's Guides along with the books that you choose.

- **LEVEL O** *Ants of All Kinds* (Vocabulary Reader) INFORMATIONAL TEXT
- **LEVEL P** *The Lives of Social Insects* INFORMATIONAL TEXT
- **LEVEL S** *Arthropods Rule!* INFORMATIONAL TEXT
- **LEVEL S** *Arthropods Everywhere!* (Language Support) INFORMATIONAL TEXT
- **LEVEL T** *Love Those Bugs!* INFORMATIONAL TEXT

For strategic intervention, use the Write-In Reader: *Busy Bees.*

Small-Group Links

- *Text and Graphic Features; Question* COMPREHENSION
- *Recognizing Suffixes* DECODING
- *Stress* FLUENCY
- *Suffixes -able, -ible* VOCABULARY STRATEGIES

Literature Discussion

You may want to call together small groups for literature discussion. See pp. 122–125 for suggested trade book titles.

Independent

Options for Independent Work

- Independent Reading
- Word Study
- Vocabulary in Context Cards 131–140
- Listening Center: respond in Reader's Notebook
- Reader's Notebook: see writing prompt
- Ready-Made Work Stations, Lesson 14: Comprehension and Fluency, Word Study, Think and Write

See Teacher's Edition Lesson 14 for more independent activity options.

Writing About Reading

- Prompt: *Wicked Wind* describes a kind of storm called a tornado. Think of a storm you have experienced. What did the storm look and sound like? How did you feel about the storm?
- Have students use their Reader's Notebook to record reactions to the literature they read and listened to this week.

GROUP SHARE Wrap up each day's Readers' Workshop by asking students to share how they applied the minilesson principle to their independent reading. Look for the Group Share section at the end of each minilesson.

Suggested Weekly Focus

Lesson 15

Whole Group

Interactive Read-Aloud/ Shared Reading

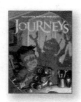

- *Ecology for Kids* by Federico Arana, Student Book: Lesson 15 INFORMATIONAL TEXT
- *Forests Are Forever*, Teacher's Edition: Lesson 15 INFORMATIONAL TEXT
- *Wonderful Weather*, Student Book: Lesson 15 POETRY

Whole-Group Links

You may use the suggested links to teach and reinforce skills in shared reading.

- *Three-Syllable Words* DECODING
- *Introduce Vocabulary (Vocabulary in Context Cards 141–150)* WORD STUDY
- *Multiple-Meaning Words* VOCABULARY STRATEGIES

Reading Minilessons

- Main Ideas and Details: Using Details to Identify Main Idea, p. 68
- Main Ideas and Details: Main Idea May Be Stated or Unstated, p. 69
- Genre: Poetry, p. 69

Use the minilessons in this guide as a bridge between shared reading experiences and guided/ independent reading.

Small Group

Guided Reading

Select texts according to your students' instructional level. You may use the books below or select from the Leveled Readers Database, pp. 112–121. For instructional support, use the Leveled Readers Teacher's Guides along with the books that you choose.

- **LEVEL N** *Squash in the Schoolyard* (Vocabulary Reader) INFORMATIONAL TEXT
- **LEVEL O** *The Seal Who Wanted to Live* FANTASY
- **LEVEL O** *The Princess and the Manatee* FANTASY
- **LEVEL P** *A Father's Garden* (Language Support) FICTION
- **LEVEL Q** *Dad's Garden* FICTION

For strategic intervention, use the Write-In Reader: *Where Have All the Frogs Gone?*

Small-Group Links

- *Main Ideas and Details; Monitor/Clarify* COMPREHENSION
- *Three-Syllable Words* DECODING
- *Expression* FLUENCY
- *Multiple-Meaning Words* VOCABULARY STRATEGIES

Literature Discussion

You may want to call together small groups for literature discussion. See pp. 122–125 for suggested trade book titles.

Independent

Options for Independent Work

- Independent Reading
- Word Study
- Vocabulary in Context Cards 141–150
- Listening Center: respond in Reader's Notebook
- Reader's Notebook: see writing prompt
- Ready-Made Work Stations, Lesson 15: Comprehension and Fluency, Word Study, Think and Write

See Teacher's Edition Lesson 15 for more independent activity options.

Writing About Reading

- Prompt: *Ecology for Kids* tells about our environment and the plants and animals that live in it. What important things did you learn about our environment? Make a list of your ideas.
- Have students use their Reader's Notebook to record reactions to the literature they read and listened to this week.

GROUP SHARE Wrap up each day's Readers' Workshop by asking students to share how they applied the minilesson principle to their independent reading. Look for the Group Share section at the end of each minilesson.

Suggested Weekly Focus

Lesson 16

Whole Group

Interactive Read-Aloud/Shared Reading

- *Riding Freedom* by Pam Muñoz Ryan, Student Book: Lesson 16 HISTORICAL FICTION
- *Getting the Story*, Teacher's Edition: Lesson 16 BIOGRAPHY
- *Spindletop*, Student Book: Lesson 16 INFORMATIONAL TEXT

Whole-Group Links

You may use the suggested links to teach and reinforce skills in shared reading.

- *Sound/Spelling Changes* DECODING
- *Introduce Vocabulary* (Vocabulary in Context Cards 151–160) WORD STUDY
- *Context Clues* VOCABULARY STRATEGIES

Reading Minilessons

- Genre: Historical Fiction, p. 70
- Genre: Biography, p. 71
- Compare and Contrast: Similarities and Differences Between Texts, p. 71

Use the minilessons in this guide as a bridge between shared reading experiences and guided/independent reading.

Small Group

Guided Reading

Select texts according to your students' instructional level. You may use the books below or select from the Leveled Readers Database, pp. 112–121. For instructional support, use the Leveled Readers Teacher's Guides along with the books that you choose.

- **LEVEL N** *Elizabeth's Stormy Ride* HISTORICAL FICTION
- **LEVEL Q** *Stagecoach Travel* (Vocabulary Reader) INFORMATIONAL TEXT
- **LEVEL S** *A Dangerous Trip* (Language Support) HISTORICAL FICTION
- **LEVEL S** *Perilous Passage* HISTORICAL FICTION
- **LEVEL S** *Come to Nicodemus* HISTORICAL FICTION

For strategic intervention, use the Write-In Reader: *The Fastest Rider in the West.*

Small-Group Links

- *Compare and Contrast; Monitor/Clarify* COMPREHENSION
- *Sound/Spelling Changes* DECODING
- *Rate* FLUENCY
- *Context Clues* VOCABULARY STRATEGIES

Literature Discussion

You may want to call together small groups for literature discussion. See pp. 122–125 for suggested trade book titles.

Independent

Options for Independent Work

- Independent Reading
- Word Study
- Vocabulary in Context Cards 151–160
- Listening Center: respond in Reader's Notebook
- Reader's Notebook: see writing prompt
- Ready-Made Work Stations, Lesson 16: Comprehension and Fluency, Word Study, Think and Write

See Teacher's Edition Lesson 16 for more independent activity options.

Writing About Reading

- Prompt: *Riding Freedom* tells the story of a girl who relearns how to drive a stagecoach after losing sight in one eye. Do you think Charlotte should have given up riding? Why or why not?
- Have students use their Reader's Notebook to record reactions to the literature they read and listened to this week.

GROUP SHARE Wrap up each day's Readers' Workshop by asking students to share how they applied the minilesson principle to their independent reading. Look for the Group Share section at the end of each minilesson.

Suggested Weekly Focus

Lesson 17

Whole Group

Interactive Read-Aloud/ Shared Reading

- *The Right Dog for the Job: Ira's Path from Service Dog to Guide Dog* by Dorothy Hinshaw Patent, Student Book: Lesson 17 NARRATIVE NONFICTION
- *Let Me Be Brave*, Teacher's Edition: Lesson 17 BIOGRAPHY
- *The Sticky Coyote* retold by Kate McGovern, Student Book: Lesson 17 TRICKSTER TALE

Whole-Group Links

You may use the suggested links to teach and reinforce skills in shared reading.

- *More Sound/Spelling Changes* DECODING
- *Introduce Vocabulary (Vocabulary in Context Cards 161–170)* WORD STUDY
- *Suffixes -ion, -ation, -ition* VOCABULARY STRATEGIES

Reading Minilessons

- Sequence of Events: Organization of Text, p. 72
- Sequence of Events: Using Clue Words, p. 73
- Genre: Trickster Tale, p. 73

Use the minilessons in this guide as a bridge between shared reading experiences and guided/independent reading.

Small Group

Guided Reading

Select texts according to your students' instructional level. You may use the books below or select from the Leveled Readers Database, pp. 112–121. For instructional support, use the Leveled Readers Teacher's Guides along with the books that you choose.

- **LEVEL N** *Animals Helping People* (Vocabulary Reader) INFORMATIONAL TEXT
- **LEVEL N** *Animal Doctors* NARRATIVE NONFICTION
- **LEVEL R** *Taking Care of Animals* (Language Support) NARRATIVE NONFICTION
- **LEVEL R** *A Rural Veterinarian* NARRATIVE NONFICTION
- **LEVEL T** *Helping Wild Animals* NARRATIVE NONFICTION

For strategic intervention, use the Write-In Reader: *Monkey Business*.

Small-Group Links

- *Sequence of Events; Summarize* COMPREHENSION
- *More Sound/Spelling Changes* DECODING
- *Intonation* FLUENCY
- *Suffixes -ion, -ation, -ition* VOCABULARY STRATEGIES

Literature Discussion

You may want to call together small groups for literature discussion. See pp. 122–125 for suggested trade book titles.

Independent

Options for Independent Work

- Independent Reading
- Word Study
- Vocabulary in Context Cards 161–170
- Listening Center: respond in Reader's Notebook
- Reader's Notebook: see writing prompt
- Ready-Made Work Stations, Lesson 17: Comprehension and Fluency, Word Study, Think and Write

See Teacher's Edition Lesson 17 for more independent activity options.

Writing About Reading

- Prompt: *The Sticky Coyote* is a play about a trickster named Coyote. What lesson does Coyote learn in the play? How can this lesson be used in your life?
- Have students use their Reader's Notebook to record reactions to the literature they read and listened to this week.

GROUP SHARE Wrap up each day's Readers' Workshop by asking students to share how they applied the minilesson principle to their independent reading. Look for the Group Share section at the end of each minilesson.

Suggested Weekly Focus

Lesson 18

Whole Group

Interactive Read-Aloud/ Shared Reading

- *Moon Runner* by Carolyn Marsden, Student Book: Lesson 18 REALISTIC FICTION
- *Darnell Tries Harder*, Teacher's Edition: Lesson 18 REALISTIC FICTION
- *A Day for the Moon*, Student Book: Lesson 18 INFORMATIONAL TEXT

Whole-Group Links

You may use the suggested links to teach and reinforce skills in shared reading.

- *Recognizing Prefixes* DECODING
- *Introduce Vocabulary (Vocabulary in Context Cards 171–180)* WORD STUDY
- *Homophones, Homonyms, Homographs* VOCABULARY STRATEGIES

Reading Minilessons

- Understanding Characters: How Characters Change, p. 74
- Compare and Contrast: Similarities and Differences in Characters, p. 75
- Compare and Contrast: Using Personal Experiences, p. 75

Use the minilessons in this guide as a bridge between shared reading experiences and guided/ independent reading.

Small Group

Guided Reading

Select texts according to your students' instructional level. You may use the books below or select from the Leveled Readers Database, pp. 112–121. For instructional support, use the Leveled Readers Teacher's Guides along with the books that you choose.

- **LEVEL N** *Tammy's Goal* REALISTIC FICTION
- **LEVEL O** *The First Lady of Track* (Vocabulary Reader) INFORMATIONAL TEXT
- **LEVEL P** *Baseball Friends* (Language Support) REALISTIC FICTION
- **LEVEL P** *Baseball Boys* REALISTIC FICTION
- **LEVEL S** *The Friendship Garden* REALISTIC FICTION

For strategic intervention, use the Write-In Reader: *Right on Track*.

Small-Group Links

- *Understanding Characters; Question* COMPREHENSION
- *Recognizing Prefixes* DECODING
- *Accuracy and Self-Correction* FLUENCY
- *Homophones, Homonyms, Homographs* VOCABULARY STRATEGIES

Literature Discussion

You may want to call together small groups for literature discussion. See pp. 122–125 for suggested trade book titles.

Independent

Options for Independent Work

- Independent Reading
- Word Study
- Vocabulary in Context Cards 171–180
- Listening Center: respond in Reader's Notebook
- Reader's Notebook: see writing prompt
- Ready-Made Work Stations, Lesson 18: Comprehension and Fluency, Word Study, Think and Write

See Teacher's Edition Lesson 18 for more independent activity options.

Writing About Reading

- Prompt: In *Darnell Tries Harder*, Darnell finally is able to ride his bike up a big hill. How do you think Darnell feels? Write about it.
- Have students use their Reader's Notebook to record reactions to the literature they read and listened to this week.

GROUP SHARE Wrap up each day's Readers' Workshop by asking students to share how they applied the minilesson principle to their independent reading. Look for the Group Share section at the end of each minilesson.

Suggested Weekly Focus

Lesson 19

Whole Group

Interactive Read-Aloud/Shared Reading

- *Harvesting Hope: The Story of Cesar Chavez* by Kathleen Krull, Student Book: Lesson 19 BIOGRAPHY
- *The Father of India*, Teacher's Edition: Lesson 19 BIOGRAPHY
- *The Edible Schoolyard* by Ned L. Legol, Student Book: Lesson 19 INFORMATIONAL TEXT

Whole-Group Links

You may use the suggested links to teach and reinforce skills in shared reading.

- *More Common Suffixes* DECODING
- *Introduce Vocabulary (Vocabulary in Context Cards 181–190)* WORD STUDY
- *Use a Dictionary* VOCABULARY STRATEGIES

Reading Minilessons

- Genre: Biography, p. 76
- Persuasion: Demonstrating Importance of the Subject, p. 77
- Genre: Informational Text, p. 77

Use the minilessons in this guide as a bridge between shared reading experiences and guided/independent reading.

Small Group

Guided Reading

Select texts according to your students' instructional level. You may use the books below or select from the Leveled Readers Database, pp. 112–121. For instructional support, use the Leveled Readers Teacher's Guides along with the books that you choose.

- **LEVEL P** *Songs for the People* BIOGRAPHY
- **LEVEL R** *A President for the People* (Language Support) BIOGRAPHY
- **LEVEL R** *The People's President* BIOGRAPHY
- **LEVEL S** *Tough Times* (Vocabulary Reader) INFORMATIONAL TEXT
- **LEVEL U** *The Story of Dorothea Lange* BIOGRAPHY

For strategic intervention, use the Write-In Reader: *Harriet Tubman: American Hero*.

Small-Group Links

- *Persuasion; Infer/Predict* COMPREHENSION
- *More Common Suffixes* DECODING
- *Stress* FLUENCY
- *Use a Dictionary* VOCABULARY STRATEGIES

Literature Discussion

You may want to call together small groups for literature discussion. See pp. 122–125 for suggested trade book titles.

Independent

Options for Independent Work

- Independent Reading
- Word Study
- Vocabulary in Context Cards 181–190
- Listening Center: respond in Reader's Notebook
- Reader's Notebook: see writing prompt
- Ready-Made Work Stations, Lesson 19: Comprehension and Fluency, Word Study, Think and Write

See Teacher's Edition Lesson 19 for more independent activity options.

Writing About Reading

- Prompt: Cesar Chavez organizes a march in *Harvesting Hope: The Story of Cesar Chavez*. Make a poster Cesar could have displayed to encourage farm workers to join him.
- Have students use their Reader's Notebook to record reactions to the literature they read and listened to this week.

GROUP SHARE Wrap up each day's Readers' Workshop by asking students to share how they applied the minilesson principle to their independent reading. Look for the Group Share section at the end of each minilesson.

Suggested Weekly Focus

Lesson 20

Whole Group

Interactive Read-Aloud/Shared Reading

- *Sacagawea* by Lise Erdich, Student Book: Lesson 20 BIOGRAPHY
- *Race Against Death*, Teacher's Edition: Lesson 20 NARRATIVE NONFICTION
- *Native American Nature Poetry*, Student Book: Lesson 20 POETRY

Whole-Group Links

You may use the suggested links to teach and reinforce skills in shared reading.

- *VCCV Pattern and Word Parts* DECODING
- *Introduce Vocabulary (Vocabulary in Context Cards 191–200)* WORD STUDY
- *Compound Words* VOCABULARY STRATEGIES

Reading Minilessons

- Main Ideas and Details: Using Details, p. 78
- Genre: Narrative Nonfiction, p. 79
- Genre: Poetry, p. 79

Use the minilessons in this guide as a bridge between shared reading experiences and guided/independent reading.

Small Group

Guided Reading

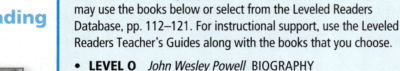

Select texts according to your students' instructional level. You may use the books below or select from the Leveled Readers Database, pp. 112–121. For instructional support, use the Leveled Readers Teacher's Guides along with the books that you choose.

- **LEVEL O** *John Wesley Powell* BIOGRAPHY
- **LEVEL Q** *Lewis and Clark's Packing List* (Vocabulary Reader) INFORMATIONAL TEXT
- **LEVEL R** *Laura Ingalls Wilder* (Language Support) BIOGRAPHY
- **LEVEL R** *Writer from the Prairie* BIOGRAPHY
- **LEVEL U** *Chief Washakie* BIOGRAPHY

For strategic intervention, use the Write-In Reader: *Conquering the Mighty Colorado*.

Small-Group Links

- *Main Ideas and Details; Visualize* COMPREHENSION
- *VCCV Pattern and Word Parts* DECODING
- *Phrasing: Punctuation* FLUENCY
- *Compound Words* VOCABULARY STRATEGIES

Literature Discussion

You may want to call together small groups for literature discussion. See pp. 122–125 for suggested trade book titles.

Independent

Options for Independent Work

- Independent Reading
- Word Study
- Vocabulary in Context Cards 191–200
- Listening Center: respond in Reader's Notebook
- Reader's Notebook: see writing prompt
- Ready-Made Work Stations, Lesson 20: Comprehension and Fluency, Word Study, Think and Write

See Teacher's Edition Lesson 20 for more independent activity options.

Writing About Reading

- Prompt: *Native American Nature Poetry* includes several nature poems written by Native Americans. Write a poem of your own that tells something about nature.
- Have students use their Reader's Notebook to record reactions to the literature they read and listened to this week.

GROUP SHARE Wrap up each day's Readers' Workshop by asking students to share how they applied the minilesson principle to their independent reading. Look for the Group Share section at the end of each minilesson.

Suggested Weekly Focus

Lesson 21

Whole Group

Interactive Read-Aloud/Shared Reading

- *The World According to Humphrey* by Betty G. Birney, Student Book: Lesson 21 FANTASY
- *Fun and Games on the Range,* Teacher's Edition: Lesson 21 INFORMATIONAL TEXT
- *Make the Switch,* Student Book: Lesson 21 ADVERTISEMENT

Whole-Group Links

You may use the suggested links to teach and reinforce skills in shared reading.

- *VCV Pattern and Word Parts* DECODING
- *Introduce Vocabulary (Vocabulary in Context Cards 201–210)* WORD STUDY
- *Multiple-Meaning Words* VOCABULARY STRATEGIES

Reading Minilessons

- Theme: Understanding the Lesson in the Story, p. 80
- Genre: Informational Text, p. 81
- Persuasion: How Authors Use Words and Visuals, p. 81

Use the minilessons in this guide as a bridge between shared reading experiences and guided/independent reading.

Small Group

Guided Reading

Select texts according to your students' instructional level. You may use the books below or select from the Leveled Readers Database, pp. 112–121. For instructional support, use the Leveled Readers Teacher's Guides along with the books that you choose.

- **LEVEL M** *The Magic of Teamwork* FANTASY
- **LEVEL Q** *Summer with Uncle Vince* (Language Support) FANTASY
- **LEVEL Q** *The Beltons' Imagination* FANTASY
- **LEVEL R** *The Truth About Rodents* (Vocabulary Reader) INFORMATIONAL TEXT
- **LEVEL S** *A Dragon's View* FANTASY

For strategic intervention, use the Write-In Reader: *Thought for the Day*.

Small-Group Links

- *Theme; Summarize* COMPREHENSION
- *VCV Pattern and Word Parts* DECODING
- *Accuracy* FLUENCY
- *Multiple-Meaning Words* VOCABULARY STRATEGIES

Literature Discussion

You may want to call together small groups for literature discussion. See pp. 122–125 for suggested trade book titles.

Independent

Options for Independent Work

- Independent Reading
- Word Study
- Vocabulary in Context Cards 201–210
- Listening Center: respond in Reader's Notebook
- Reader's Notebook: see writing prompt
- Ready-Made Work Stations, Lesson 21: Comprehension and Fluency, Word Study, Think and Write

See Teacher's Edition Lesson 21 for more independent activity options.

Writing About Reading

- Prompt: The family in *The World According to Humphrey* watches a lot of TV. Write a list of things that you can do instead of watching TV. Explain why your ideas might be better things to do for entertainment.
- Have students use their Reader's Notebook to record reactions to the literature they read and listened to this week.

GROUP SHARE Wrap up each day's Readers' Workshop by asking students to share how they applied the minilesson principle to their independent reading. Look for the Group Share section at the end of each minilesson.

Suggested Weekly Focus

Lesson 22

Whole Group

Interactive Read-Aloud/ Shared Reading

- *I Could Do That! Esther Morris Gets Women the Vote* by Linda Arms White, Student Book: Lesson 22 BIOGRAPHY
- *Jane's Big Ideas,* Teacher's Edition: Lesson 22 BIOGRAPHY
- *Working for the Vote* by Alice Cary, Student Book: Lesson 22 PLAY

Whole-Group Links

You may use the suggested links to teach and reinforce skills in shared reading.

- *Syllable Patterns and Word Parts* DECODING
- *Introduce Vocabulary (Vocabulary in Context Cards 211–220)* WORD STUDY
- *Use a Dictionary* VOCABULARY STRATEGIES

Reading Minilessons

- Cause and Effect: Multiple Causes for One Effect, p. 82
- Cause and Effect: How Big Ideas Cause Changes, p. 83
- Genre: Play, p. 83

Use the minilessons in this guide as a bridge between shared reading experiences and guided/ independent reading.

Small Group

Guided Reading

Select texts according to your students' instructional level. You may use the books below or select from the Leveled Readers Database, pp. 112–121. For instructional support, use the Leveled Readers Teacher's Guides along with the books that you choose.

- **LEVEL P** *The First Woman Doctor* BIOGRAPHY
- **LEVEL S** *Mill Girls* (Vocabulary Reader) INFORMATIONAL TEXT
- **LEVEL S** *Shirley Chisholm* (Language Support) BIOGRAPHY
- **LEVEL S** *A Champion of Change* BIOGRAPHY
- **LEVEL U** *The Writer Who Changed America* BIOGRAPHY

For strategic intervention, use the Write-In Reader: *Getting the Vote.*

Small-Group Links

- *Cause and Effect; Infer/Predict* COMPREHENSION
- *Syllable Patterns and Word Parts* DECODING
- *Phrasing: Pauses* FLUENCY
- *Use a Dictionary* VOCABULARY STRATEGIES

Literature Discussion

You may want to call together small groups for literature discussion. See pp. 122–125 for suggested trade book titles.

Independent

Options for Independent Work

- Independent Reading
- Word Study
- Vocabulary in Context Cards 211–220
- Listening Center: respond in Reader's Notebook
- Reader's Notebook: see writing prompt
- Ready-Made Work Stations, Lesson 22: Comprehension and Fluency, Word Study, Think and Write

See Teacher's Edition Lesson 22 for more independent activity options.

Writing About Reading

- **Prompt:** *Jane's Big Ideas* tells about the life of Jane Addams. Jane believed that women should have the right to vote. Write a short speech telling others why women should have the right to vote.
- Have students use their Reader's Notebook to record reactions to the literature they read and listened to this week.

GROUP SHARE Wrap up each day's Readers' Workshop by asking students to share how they applied the minilesson principle to their independent reading. Look for the Group Share section at the end of each minilesson.

Suggested Weekly Focus

Lesson 23

Whole Group

Interactive Read-Aloud/ Shared Reading

- *The Ever-Living Tree: The Life and Times of a Coast Redwood* by Linda Vieira, Student Book: Lesson 23 INFORMATIONAL TEXT
- *Deserts on the Move?* Teacher's Edition: Lesson 23 INFORMATIONAL TEXT
- *Towering Trees*, Student Book: Lesson 23 POETRY

Whole-Group Links

You may use the suggested links to teach and reinforce skills in shared reading.

- *Difficult VCCV Patterns* DECODING
- *Introduce Vocabulary (Vocabulary in Context Cards 221–230)* WORD STUDY
- *Prefixes* pre-, inter-, ex- VOCABULARY STRATEGIES

Reading Minilessons

- Text and Graphic Features: Relating Visuals to Text, p. 84
- Cause and Effect: How Authors Explain, p. 85
- Genre: Poetry, p. 85

Use the minilessons in this guide as a bridge between shared reading experiences and guided/independent reading.

Small Group

Guided Reading

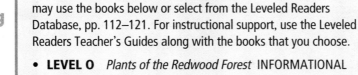

Select texts according to your students' instructional level. You may use the books below or select from the Leveled Readers Database, pp. 112–121. For instructional support, use the Leveled Readers Teacher's Guides along with the books that you choose.

- **LEVEL O** *Plants of the Redwood Forest* INFORMATIONAL TEXT
- **LEVEL P** *Forever Green* (Vocabulary Reader) INFORMATIONAL TEXT
- **LEVEL S** *Animals of the Redwood Forest* (Language Support) INFORMATIONAL TEXT
- **LEVEL S** *Life Among the Redwoods* INFORMATIONAL TEXT
- **LEVEL S** *Gentle Redwood Giants* INFORMATIONAL TEXT

For strategic intervention, use the Write-In Reader: *Exploring Redwood Park*.

Small-Group Links

- *Text and Graphic Features; Monitor/Clarify* COMPREHENSION
- *Difficult VCCV Patterns* DECODING
- *Stress* FLUENCY
- *Prefixes* pre-, inter-, ex- VOCABULARY STRATEGIES

Literature Discussion

You may want to call together small groups for literature discussion. See pp. 122–125 for suggested trade book titles.

Independent

Options for Independent Work

- Independent Reading
- Word Study
- Vocabulary in Context Cards 221–230
- Listening Center: respond in Reader's Notebook
- Reader's Notebook: see writing prompt
- Ready-Made Work Stations, Lesson 23: Comprehension and Fluency, Word Study, Think and Write

See Teacher's Edition Lesson 23 for more independent activity options.

Writing About Reading

- Prompt: The poems in *Towering Trees* tell about different trees and what they are like. Write a poem about a tree in your neighborhood or one you have seen.
- Have students use their Reader's Notebook to record reactions to the literature they read and listened to this week.

GROUP SHARE Wrap up each day's Readers' Workshop by asking students to share how they applied the minilesson principle to their independent reading. Look for the Group Share section at the end of each minilesson.

Suggested Weekly Focus

Lesson 24

Whole Group

Interactive Read-Aloud/Shared Reading

- *Owen and Mzee: The True Story of a Remarkable Friendship* by Isabella Hatkoff, Craig Hatkoff, and Dr. Paula Kahumbu, Student Book: Lesson 24 NARRATIVE NONFICTION
- *New Friends in the Newsroom,* Teacher's Edition: Lesson 24 REALISTIC FICTION
- *Sea Sanctuary* by Rob Hale, Student Book: Lesson 24 INFORMATIONAL TEXT

Whole-Group Links

You may use the suggested links to teach and reinforce skills in shared reading.

- *VCCCV Pattern* DECODING
- *Introduce Vocabulary (Vocabulary in Context Cards* 231–240) WORD STUDY
- *Suffixes* -ed, -ly VOCABULARY STRATEGIES

Reading Minilessons

- Compare and Contrast: Comparing Ideas, p. 86
- Genre: Realistic Fiction, p. 87
- Summarize: Understanding a Text, p. 87

Use the minilessons in this guide as a bridge between shared reading experiences and guided/independent reading.

Small Group

Guided Reading

Select texts according to your students' instructional level. You may use the books below or select from the Leveled Readers Database, pp. 112–121. For instructional support, use the Leveled Readers Teacher's Guides along with the books that you choose.

- **LEVEL P** *Flying into History* NARRATIVE NONFICTION
- **LEVEL P** *Dangerous Waves* (Vocabulary Reader) INFORMATIONAL TEXT
- **LEVEL S** *Helen Keller's Special Friend* (Language Support) NARRATIVE NONFICTION
- **LEVEL S** *Helen Keller's Lifelong Friend* NARRATIVE NONFICTION
- **LEVEL S** *Champions on Ice* NARRATIVE NONFICTION

For strategic intervention, use the Write-In Reader: *A Cool Cat.*

Small-Group Links

- *Compare and Contrast; Analyze/Evaluate* COMPREHENSION
- *VCCCV Pattern* DECODING
- *Intonation* FLUENCY
- *Suffixes* -ed, -ly VOCABULARY STRATEGIES

Literature Discussion

You may want to call together small groups for literature discussion. See pp. 122–125 for suggested trade book titles.

Independent

Options for Independent Work

- Independent Reading
- Word Study
- Vocabulary in Context Cards 231–240
- Listening Center: respond in Reader's Notebook
- Reader's Notebook: see writing prompt
- Ready-Made Work Stations, Lesson 24: Comprehension and Fluency, Word Study, Think and Write

See Teacher's Edition Lesson 24 for more independent activity options.

Writing About Reading

- Prompt: The story of the two animal friends in *Owen and Mzee: The True Story of a Remarkable Friendship* has been told in many newspapers. Write a newspaper article of your own to tell about these two amazing animals.
- Have students use their Reader's Notebook to record reactions to the literature they read and listened to this week.

GROUP SHARE Wrap up each day's Readers' Workshop by asking students to share how they applied the minilesson principle to their independent reading. Look for the Group Share section at the end of each minilesson.

Suggested Weekly Focus

Lesson 25

Whole Group

Interactive Read-Aloud/Shared Reading

- *The Fun They Had* by Isaac Asimov, Student Book: Lesson 25 SCIENCE FICTION
- *The Future of Flight,* Teacher's Edition: Lesson 25 INFORMATIONAL TEXT
- *Technology for All Learners* by Mia Vosic, Student Book: Lesson 25 INFORMATIONAL TEXT

Whole-Group Links

You may use the suggested links to teach and reinforce skills in shared reading.

- *VV Pattern* DECODING
- *Introduce Vocabulary (Vocabulary in Context Cards 241–250)* WORD STUDY
- *Greek and Latin Word Parts* meter, therm, aud, fac VOCABULARY STRATEGIES

Reading Minilessons

- Author's Purpose: Using Details, p. 88
- Genre: Informational Text, p. 89
- Summarize: Understanding a Text, p. 89

Use the minilessons in this guide as a bridge between shared reading experiences and guided/independent reading.

Small Group

Guided Reading

Select texts according to your students' instructional level. You may use the books below or select from the Leveled Readers Database, pp. 112–121. For instructional support, use the Leveled Readers Teacher's Guides along with the books that you choose.

- **LEVEL M** *The Linney Twins Get Cooking* SCIENCE FICTION
- **LEVEL P** *Remarkable Robots* (Vocabulary Reader) INFORMATIONAL TEXT
- **LEVEL S** *Dex Is a Hero* (Language Support) SCIENCE FICTION
- **LEVEL S** *A Hero Weighs In* SCIENCE FICTION
- **LEVEL T** *Math Today and Tomorrow* SCIENCE FICTION

For strategic intervention, use the Write-In Reader: *The Kirks*.

Small-Group Links

- *Author's Purpose; Question* COMPREHENSION
- *VV Pattern* DECODING
- *Adjust Rate to Purpose* FLUENCY
- *Greek and Latin Word Parts* meter, therm, aud, fac VOCABULARY STRATEGIES

Literature Discussion

You may want to call together small groups for literature discussion. See pp. 122–125 for suggested trade book titles.

Independent

Options for Independent Work

- Independent Reading
- Word Study
- Vocabulary in Context Cards 241–250
- Listening Center: respond in Reader's Notebook
- Reader's Notebook: see writing prompt
- Ready-Made Work Stations, Lesson 25: Comprehension and Fluency, Word Study, Think and Write

See Teacher's Edition Lesson 25 for more independent activity options.

Writing About Reading

- Prompt: *The Fun They Had* tells about students far in the future. Would you like to go to a school like the one in the story? Tell why or why not.
- Have students use their Reader's Notebook to record reactions to the literature they read and listened to this week.

GROUP SHARE Wrap up each day's Readers' Workshop by asking students to share how they applied the minilesson principle to their independent reading. Look for the Group Share section at the end of each minilesson.

Suggested Weekly Focus

Lesson 26

Whole Group

Interactive Read-Aloud/Shared Reading

- *The Girl Who Loved Spiders* by Karen Halvorsen Schreck, Student Magazine: Lesson 26 REALISTIC FICTION
- *Web Wise* by Margaret Hall, Student Magazine: Lesson 26 INFORMATIONAL TEXT
- Poetry Place
  "The Spider" by Jack Prelutsky, Student Magazine: Lesson 26 POETRY
  "Spider Ropes" by James Berry, Student Magazine: Lesson 26 POETRY

Whole-Group Links

You may use the suggested links to teach and reinforce skills in shared reading.

- *Common Final Syllables* DECODING
- *Vocabulary (Vocabulary in Context Cards 5, 9, 14, 15, 23, 29, 31, 38, 46, 48)* WORD STUDY
- *Greek and Latin Roots* VOCABULARY STRATEGIES

Reading Minilessons

- Story Structure: Problem and Solution, p. 90
- Genre: Informational Text, p. 91
- Genre: Poetry, p. 91

Use the minilessons in this guide as a bridge between shared reading experiences and guided/independent reading.

Small Group

Guided Reading

Select texts according to your students' instructional level. You may use the novels below or select from the Leveled Readers Database, pp. 112–121. For instructional support, use the Leveled Readers Teacher's Guides along with the books that you choose.

- **LEVEL P** *Justin and the Best Biscuits in the World* by Mildred Pitts Walter, pp. 1–27 REALISTIC FICTION
- **LEVEL P** *Phineas L. MacGuire . . . Gets Slimed!* by Frances O'Roark Dowell, pp. 1–38 REALISTIC FICTION
- **LEVEL V** *Sea Turtles: Ocean Nomads* by Mary M. Cerullo, pp. 5–10 INFORMATIONAL TEXT

For strategic intervention, use the Write-In Reader: *Coming Home*.

Small-Group Links

- *Story Structure; Visualize* COMPREHENSION
- *Greek and Latin Roots* VOCABULARY STRATEGIES

Literature Discussion

You may want to call together small groups for literature discussion. See pp. 122–125 for suggested trade book titles.

Independent

Options for Independent Work

- Independent Reading
- Word Study
- Vocabulary in Context Cards 5, 9, 14, 15, 23, 29, 31, 38, 46, 48
- Reader's Notebook: see writing prompt

See Teacher's Edition Lesson 26 for more independent activity options.

Writing About Reading

- Prompt: *The Girl Who Loved Spiders* gives information about spiders while also telling a story. Which of the spiders mentioned did you find most interesting and why?
- Have students use their Reader's Notebook to record reactions to the literature they read and listened to this week.

GROUP SHARE Wrap up each day's Readers' Workshop by asking students to share how they applied the minilesson principle to their independent reading. Look for the Group Share section at the end of each minilesson.

Suggested Weekly Focus

Lesson 27

Whole Group

Interactive Read-Aloud/Shared Reading

- *Amphibian Alert!* by Elliott Meiner, Student Magazine: Lesson 27 INFORMATIONAL TEXT
- *The Frog in the Milk Pail* retold by M. C. Hall, Student Magazine: Lesson 27 FABLE
- Poetry Place

  "Toad by the Road" by Joanne Ryder, Student Magazine: Lesson 27 POETRY

  "The Poison-Dart Frogs" by Douglas Florian, Student Magazine: Lesson 27 POETRY

Whole-Group Links

You may use the suggested links to teach and reinforce skills in shared reading.

- *More Final Syllables* DECODING
- *Vocabulary* (Vocabulary in Context Cards 28, 47, 49, 63, 122, 138, 148, 205, 227, 228) WORD STUDY
- *Analogies* VOCABULARY STRATEGIES

Reading Minilessons

- Main Ideas and Details: Stated or Unstated Main Idea, p. 92
- Genre: Fable, p. 93
- Genre: Poetry, p. 93

Use the minilessons in this guide as a bridge between shared reading experiences and guided/independent reading.

Small Group

Guided Reading

Select texts according to your students' instructional level. You may use the novels below or select from the Leveled Readers Database, pp. 112–121. For instructional support, use the Leveled Reader's Teachers Guides along with the books that you choose.

- **LEVEL P** *Justin and the Best Biscuits in the World* by Mildred Pitts Walter, pp. 28–48 REALISTIC FICTION
- **LEVEL P** *Phineas L. MacGuire . . . Gets Slimed!* by Frances O'Roark Dowell, pp. 39–75 REALISTIC FICTION
- **LEVEL V** *Sea Turtles: Ocean Nomads* by Mary M. Cerullo, pp. 11–18 INFORMATIONAL TEXT

For strategic intervention, use the Write-In Reader: *The Life of a Pond.*

Small-Group Links

- *Main Ideas/Supporting Details; Question* COMPREHENSION
- *Analogies* VOCABULARY STRATEGIES

Literature Discussion

You may want to call together small groups for literature discussion. See pp. 122–125 for suggested trade book titles.

Independent

Options for Independent Work

- Independent Reading
- Word Study
- Vocabulary in Context Cards 28, 47, 49, 63, 122, 138, 148, 205, 227, 228
- Reader's Notebook: see writing prompt

See Teacher's Edition Lesson 27 for more independent activity options.

Writing About Reading

- Prompt: *Amphibian Alert!* tells about different reasons that amphibians are disappearing. Make a poster to tell others about ways to protect amphibians.
- Have students use their Reader's Notebook to record reactions to the literature they read and listened to this week.

GROUP SHARE Wrap up each day's Readers' Workshop by asking students to share how they applied the minilesson principle to their independent reading. Look for the Group Share section at the end of each minilesson.

Lesson 27 • **35**

Suggested Weekly Focus

Lesson 28

Whole Group

Interactive Read-Aloud/Shared Reading

- *Museums: Worlds of Wonder* by Jody Cosson, Student Magazine: Lesson 28 EXPOSITORY NONFICTION
- *Making the Most from Trash* by H. G. Ellis, Student Magazine: Lesson 28 PHOTO ESSAY
- Poetry Place

  "Dinosaur Bone" by Alice Schertle, Student Magazine: Lesson 28 POETRY

  "Museum Farewell" by Rebecca Kai Dotlich, Student Magazine: Lesson 28 POETRY

Whole-Group Links

You may use the suggested links to teach and reinforce skills in shared reading.

- *Stress in Multi-Syllable Words* DECODING
- *Vocabulary (Vocabulary in Context Cards 85, 87, 97, 104, 106, 121, 130, 139, 143, 145)* WORD STUDY
- *Prefixes* con-, com-, in-, im- VOCABULARY STRATEGIES

Reading Minilessons

- Fact and Opinion: Differences Between Facts and Opinions, p. 94
- Fact and Opinion: Supporting Opinions with Facts, p. 95
- Genre: Poetry, p. 95

Use the minilessons in this guide as a bridge between shared reading experiences and guided/independent reading.

Small Group

Guided Reading

Select texts according to your students' instructional level. You may use the novels below or select from the Leveled Readers Database, pp. 112–121. For instructional support, use the Leveled Readers Teacher's Guides along with the books that you choose.

- **LEVEL P** *Justin and the Best Biscuits in the World* by Mildred Pitts Walter, pp. 49–77 REALISTIC FICTION
- **LEVEL P** *Phineas L. MacGuire . . . Gets Slimed!* by Frances O'Roark Dowell, pp. 76–109 REALISTIC FICTION
- **LEVEL V** *Sea Turtles: Ocean Nomads* by Mary M. Cerullo, pp. 19–25 INFORMATIONAL TEXT

For strategic intervention, use the Write-In Reader: *In the Museum*.

Small-Group Links

- *Fact and Opinion; Monitor/Clarify* COMPREHENSION
- *Prefixes* con-, com-, in-, im- VOCABULARY STRATEGIES

Literature Discussion

You may want to call together small groups for literature discussion. See pp. 122–125 for suggested trade book titles.

Independent

Options for Independent Work

- Independent Reading
- Word Study
- Vocabulary in Context Cards 85, 87, 97, 104, 106, 121, 130, 139, 143, 145
- Reader's Notebook: see writing prompt

See Teacher's Edition Lesson 28 for more independent activity options.

Writing About Reading

- Prompt: *Museums: Worlds of Wonder* tells about a number of different museums. Tell which one you would like to visit, and tell why.
- Have students use their Reader's Notebook to record reactions to the literature they read and listened to this week.

GROUP SHARE Wrap up each day's Readers' Workshop by asking students to share how they applied the minilesson principle to their independent reading. Look for the Group Share section at the end of each minilesson.

Suggested Weekly Focus

Lesson 29

Whole Group

Interactive Read-Aloud/Shared Reading

- *Save Timber Woods!* by Lillian Dietrich, Student Magazine: Lesson 29 PLAY
- *John Muir: A Persuasive Essay* by Delia Greve, Student Magazine: Lesson 29 PERSUASION
- Poetry Place
  "The Comb of Trees" by Claudia Lewis, Student Magazine: Lesson 29 POETRY
  "Enjoy the Earth" from Yoruba, Africa, Student Magazine: Lesson 29 POETRY

Whole-Group Links

You may use the suggested links to teach and reinforce skills in shared reading.

- *Silent Consonants* DECODING
- *Vocabulary* (Vocabulary in Context Cards 159, 160, 163, 166, 175, 179, 186, 190, 191, 193) WORD STUDY
- *Word Origins* VOCABULARY STRATEGIES

Reading Minilessons

- Understanding Characters: Reasons for Characters' Actions, p. 96
- Persuasion: Understanding the Author's Message, p. 97
- Genre: Poetry, p. 97

Use the minilessons in this guide as a bridge between shared reading experiences and guided/independent reading.

Small Group

Guided Reading

Select texts according to your students' instructional level. You may use the novels below or select from the Leveled Readers Database, pp. 112–121. For instructional support, use the Leveled Readers Teacher's Guides along with the books that you choose.

- **LEVEL P** *Justin and the Best Biscuits in the World* by Mildred Pitts Walter, pp. 78–94 REALISTIC FICTION
- **LEVEL P** *Phineas L. MacGuire . . . Gets Slimed!* by Frances O'Roark Dowell, pp. 110–150 REALISTIC FICTION
- **LEVEL V** *Sea Turtles: Ocean Nomads* by Mary M. Cerullo, pp. 26–30 INFORMATIONAL TEXT

For strategic intervention, use the Write-In Reader: *A Stop in the Desert.*

Small-Group Links

- *Understanding Characters; Infer/Predict* COMPREHENSION
- *Word Origins* VOCABULARY STRATEGIES

Literature Discussion

You may want to call together small groups for literature discussion. See pp. 122–125 for suggested trade book titles.

Independent

Options for Independent Work

- Independent Reading
- Word Study
- Vocabulary in Context Cards 159, 160, 163, 166, 175, 179, 186, 190, 191, 193
- Reader's Notebook: see writing prompt

See Teacher's Edition Lesson 29 for more independent activity options.

Writing About Reading

- Prompt: *Following Muir: A Persuasive Essay* tells different ways to follow John Muir's example. Tell which way you would choose, and explain why.
- Have students use their Reader's Notebook to record reactions to the literature they read and listened to this week.

GROUP SHARE Wrap up each day's Readers' Workshop by asking students to share how they applied the minilesson principle to their independent reading. Look for the Group Share section at the end of each minilesson.

Suggested Weekly Focus

Lesson 30

Whole Group

Interactive Read-Aloud/Shared Reading

- *Mystery at Reed's Pond* by Zoe Zolbrod, Student Magazine: Lesson 30 MYSTERY
- *A Big Python Problem* by Trillio DeBernardi, Student Magazine: Lesson 30 INFORMATIONAL TEXT
- Poetry Place
  "Naming the Turtle" by Patricia Hubbell, Student Magazine: Lesson 30 POETRY
  "Greater Flamingo" by Tony Johnston, Student Magazine: Lesson 30 POETRY

Whole-Group Links

You may use the suggested links to teach and reinforce skills in shared reading.

- *Unusual Spellings* DECODING
- *Vocabulary (Vocabulary in Context Cards 201, 208, 219, 220, 221, 224, 232, 241, 248, 250)* WORD STUDY
- *Suffixes* -er, -or, -ist VOCABULARY STRATEGIES

Reading Minilessons

- Conclusions: Using Details, p. 98
- Genre: Informational Text, p. 99
- Genre: Poetry, p. 99

Use the minilessons in this guide as a bridge between shared reading experiences and guided/independent reading.

Small Group

Guided Reading

Select texts according to your students' instructional level. You may use the novels below or select from the Leveled Readers Database, pp. 112–121. For instructional support, use the Leveled Readers Teacher's Guides along with the books that you choose.

- **LEVEL P** *Justin and the Best Biscuits in the World* by Mildred Pitts Walter, pp. 95–177 REALISTIC FICTION
- **LEVEL P** *Phineas L. MacGuire . . . Gets Slimed!* by Frances O'Roark Dowell, pp. 151–197 REALISTIC FICTION
- **LEVEL V** *Sea Turtles: Ocean Nomads* by Mary M. Cerullo, pp. 31–38 INFORMATIONAL TEXT

For strategic intervention, use the Write-In Reader: *A Boat in the Wilderness*.

Small-Group Links

- *Conclusions/Generalizations; Summarize* COMPREHENSION
- *Suffixes* -er, -or, -ist VOCABULARY STRATEGIES

Literature Discussion

You may want to call together small groups for literature discussion. See pp. 122–125 for suggested trade book titles.

Independent

Options for Independent Work

- Independent Reading
- Word Study
- Vocabulary in Context Cards 201, 208, 219, 220, 221, 224, 232, 241, 248, 250
- Reader's Notebook: see writing prompt

See Teacher's Edition Lesson 30 for more independent activity options.

Writing About Reading

- **Prompt:** *Mystery at Reed's Pond* tells about the problems caused when people let their pet turtles free in a pond. Write a paragraph to tell others why they shouldn't do this.
- Have students use their Reader's Notebook to record reactions to the literature they read and listened to this week.

GROUP SHARE Wrap up each day's Readers' Workshop by asking students to share how they applied the minilesson principle to their independent reading. Look for the Group Share section at the end of each minilesson.

38 • Lesson 30

Whole-Group Lessons

Whole-group lessons provide a context for all students to think about what they read, learn from their peers' ideas, and demonstrate understanding of specific skills. To prepare for each lesson sequence on the pages that follow, we suggest that you:

- Read the literature in advance, and use self-stick notes to mark the suggested stopping points. As needed, supplement with questions that address your students' needs and allow for spontaneity of your students' responses.

- Set up an easel with chart paper (or use an overhead projector or whiteboard) to display minilesson principles and to share graphic organizers that you will complete with students.

Lesson 1	40	Lesson 16	70
Lesson 2	42	Lesson 17	72
Lesson 3	44	Lesson 18	74
Lesson 4	46	Lesson 19	76
Lesson 5	48	Lesson 20	78
Lesson 6	50	Lesson 21	80
Lesson 7	52	Lesson 22	82
Lesson 8	54	Lesson 23	84
Lesson 9	56	Lesson 24	86
Lesson 10	58	Lesson 25	88
Lesson 11	60	Lesson 26	90
Lesson 12	62	Lesson 27	92
Lesson 13	64	Lesson 28	94
Lesson 14	66	Lesson 29	96
Lesson 15	68	Lesson 30	98

Whole-Group Lessons

Because of Winn-Dixie
Student Book, Lesson 1

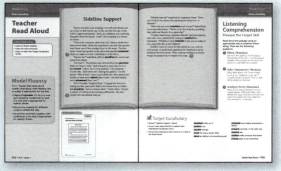

Sideline Support
Teacher's Edition, Lesson 1

Because of BookEnds
Student Book, Lesson 1

▶ Because of Winn-Dixie

INTERACTIVE READ-ALOUD/SHARED READING

Read aloud the story to students. Stop periodically for very brief discussion of the text. Use the following suggested stopping points and prompts for quick group response, or give a specific prompt and have partners or threes turn and talk.

- After Opal brings Winn-Dixie into the library, ask: "What does Miss Franny think about Winn-Dixie?" Follow-up: "How have her feelings changed?"
- After Miss Franny tells about the wild men, women, and bears, ask: "Why do you think Miss Franny keeps telling Opal about what Florida used to be like?"
- After Miss Franny sighs about her old friends, ask: "Why does Miss Franny sigh?" Follow-up: "Turn and talk with a partner about how you think Opal feels about Miss Franny."
- At the end of the story, ask: "Why is the friendship between Opal and Miss Franny important to both of them?"

MINILESSON Story Structure

TEACH Display the minilesson principle on chart paper, and read it aloud to students. Tell students that they are going to learn about how thinking about a story's events can help them understand events and what they reveal about the characters.

1. Remind students of the scene in *Because of Winn-Dixie* when the bear comes into the library. Suggested language: "A memorable scene from the story was when the bear surprised Miss Franny in the library. Why do you think the author included this scene?" *(It showed that Miss Franny wasn't afraid to stand up for herself. Telling the bear story helped her form a bond with Opal.)*

> **MINILESSON PRINCIPLE**
>
> Readers think about the important events in a story to help them understand what happens.

2. Help students connect the bear scene back to events at the beginning of the story. Suggested language: "In the beginning of the story, Miss Franny saw Winn-Dixie and thought he was a bear. How did events later in the story help you understand Miss Franny's reaction to Winn-Dixie?" *(Later events helped me understand why Miss Franny was scared of Winn-Dixie at first.)*

3. Work with students to name other important events from the story and tell how they work together to help them understand what happens. Record students' ideas in a Story Map like the one shown here.

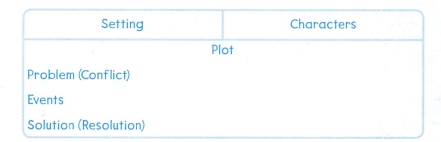

SUMMARIZE AND APPLY Restate the minilesson principle, and tell students to apply it to their independent reading. Suggested language: "When you read, think about the important events in the story and how they are connected. Think about how the events help you understand the characters and what happens in the story."

GROUP SHARE Ask students to share an important event in a story they have read. Have them explain why it was important for the author to include the scene they chose.

40 • Lesson 1

Lesson 1

▶ Sideline Support

INTERACTIVE READ-ALOUD/SHARED READING

Read aloud the story to students. Stop periodically for brief discussion of the text. Use the following suggested stopping points and prompts:

- After Brett says *Excuse me?* to Omar, ask: "Why is Brett surprised when he hears Omar speak?" (*Before then, he'd never heard Omar say anything longer than a word or two.*)
- After Brett suggests an *attitude tune-up*, say: "Brett is trying to get Omar to look at the situation in a different way. How do you think his advice will help Omar?"
- At the end of the story, say: "What lesson does Omar learn from Brett? Turn and talk about your thinking with a partner. Talk about how Brett's advice can be applied to other situations."

MINILESSON Story Structure

TEACH Display the minilesson principle on chart paper, and read it aloud to students. Tell students that they are going to learn about the problem and solution in a story.

1. Explain to students that the characters in stories often have a problem to solve. Guide students to name Omar's problem in *Sideline Support*. Suggested language: "In the beginning of the story, you found out that Omar was unhappy. What problem did Omar have?" (*He didn't have opportunities to play like his teammates.*)

> **MINILESSON PRINCIPLE**
> Readers notice the problem in the story and how it is solved.

2. Talk with students about how Brett helps Omar solve his problem. Suggested language: "Why did Omar feel better about his problem at the end of the story?" (*Brett showed him how to have a positive attitude and to appreciate a day outside with friends.*) Ask students to explain how they know the problem was solved. (*Omar smiled and jumped up to support his team.*)

3. Record students' ideas about the problem and the solution in a Story Map.

SUMMARIZE AND APPLY Restate the minilesson principle. Tell students to look for the problem and solution in a story when they read. Suggested language: "When you read, think about what problem the characters have. Then look for the solution to the problem, and think about how it was solved."

GROUP SHARE Ask students to share a problem from a story they read. Then have them tell how the problem was solved.

▶ Because of BookEnds

INTERACTIVE READ-ALOUD/SHARED READING

Read aloud the selection to students. Stop periodically for brief discussion of the text. Use the following suggested stopping points and prompts:

- After the description of the meeting the adults have, ask: "What problem did the adults have?" Follow-up: "How do you think Brandon will use his problem-solving talent to help?"
- After reading the section A Little Boy's Big Idea, ask: "What are some words you would use to describe Brandon? Turn and talk with a partner to compare your ideas."
- After reading the section BookEnds Is Born, say: "Talk with a partner about how Brandon's idea as a child has grown into something big."

MINILESSON Genre: Informational Text

TEACH Remind students that *Because of BookEnds* is informational text—it tells facts about a topic.

1. Direct students' attention to the bar graph on the last page. Tell students that authors of informational texts often use features like this one to help readers understand the author's message and to see it in a different way. Suggested language: "How does the information in the bar graph help you understand what Brett did?" (*It shows how his idea has been put into action in specific schools and how many books the schools have donated.*)

> **MINILESSON PRINCIPLE**
> Readers look for special features in informational text to help them understand the author's message.

2. Next, point out to students the numbered steps in the last section. Ask a student to read them aloud. Then ask why the steps are important. Suggested language: "What do these numbered steps explain?" (*how to hold a book drive*) Follow-up: "Why do you think the author included this section?" (*If readers were inspired by Brett's idea, the information will help them to organize book drives at their school.*)

3. Ask students to help you summarize the importance of special features in informational texts as you write the minilesson principle on chart paper.

SUMMARIZE AND APPLY Restate the minilesson principle. Tell students to look for special features in their reading. Suggested language: "When you read an informational text, look for special features that the author uses to give you information. Think about what the features help you understand about the author's message."

GROUP SHARE Ask students to share one feature from their reading and to tell how it helped them understand the author's message.

Whole-Group Lessons • 41

Whole-Group Lessons

My Brother Martin: A Sister Remembers Growing Up with the Rev. Dr. Martin Luther King Jr.
Student Book, Lesson 2

The Troublemaker Who Healed a Nation
Teacher's Edition, Lesson 2

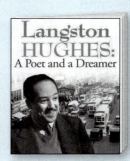

Langston Hughes: A Poet and a Dreamer
Student Book, Lesson 2

▶ My Brother Martin

INTERACTIVE READ-ALOUD/SHARED READING

Read aloud the biography to students. Stop periodically for very brief discussion of the text. Use the following suggested stopping points and prompts for quick group response, or give a specific prompt and have partners or threes turn and talk.

- After reading the first page, ask: "Who is telling this story?" (*Martin's sister*) Follow-up: "How does this make the selection more interesting to read?"
- After reading about where Martin and his family lived in Atlanta, ask: "How would you describe where Martin and his family lived?" Follow-up: "What was it like for them to live there?"
- At the end of the selection, say: "The author gives information about Martin's parents. Turn and talk with a partner about how Martin's parents were a good example for Martin."

MINILESSON Genre: Biography

TEACH Explain to students that a biography is a kind of writing that tells facts about a real person's life. Then display the minilesson principle on chart paper, and read it aloud to students. Tell students that they are going to think about what the author of *My Brother Martin* wanted them to believe and understand about the subject, or the person the biography is about.

1. Point out to students that Martin's sister told about events in Martin's childhood. Suggested language: "Almost all of this biography told about some important things that happened to Martin as a child. What were some of these events?"

2. Discuss with students that by choosing these events, the author shared information that she felt was important to know about her brother. Suggested language: "We found out that early in Martin's life, some of his friends stopped playing with him. Because of that experience, he made a promise to make changes in the world. The author wanted us to know that Martin's experiences as a child inspired him throughout his life."

3. Work with students to name other things the author wanted readers to believe and understand about Martin. Guide them to recognize that Martin's parents were a positive influence and inspired Martin to dream. Records students' ideas in a T-Map that explains events and why they were important.

> **MINILESSON PRINCIPLE**
> Readers think about what the author of a biography wants them to believe and understand about the subject.

Event	Why Event Was Important

SUMMARIZE AND APPLY Restate the minilesson principle. Then tell students to apply it to their independent reading. Suggested language: "When you read a biography, think about what the author wants you to believe and understand about the subject."

GROUP SHARE Ask students to share information from a biography they read. Have them tell what the author wanted them to believe and understand about the subject.

42 • Lesson 2

Lesson 2

▶ The Troublemaker Who Healed a Nation

INTERACTIVE READ-ALOUD/SHARED READING

Read aloud the biography to students. Stop periodically for brief discussion of the text. Use the following suggested stopping points and prompts:

- After reading the first paragraph, ask: "Why do you think a troublemaker would make an unlikely candidate for a Nobel Peace Prize?"
- After reading about Robben's Island, ask: "Why do you think the author tells you that Mandela refused special treatment in prison?"
- At the end of the selection, ask students to turn and tell a partner one reason why people respect Mandela.

MINILESSON Author's Purpose

TEACH Display the minilesson principle on chart paper, and read it aloud to students. Tell students that they are going to learn how to use the genre of a text to explain the author's purpose, or reason, for writing.

1. Remind students that the genre of *The Troublemaker Who Healed a Nation* is biography. Suggested language: "How do you know that this is a biography?" (*It gives facts about a real person named Nelson Mandela.*) Follow-up: "What did you learn about Mandela's life from this biography?"

> **MINILESSON PRINCIPLE**
>
> Readers think about the genre of a text to help them explain the author's purpose for writing.

2. Explain to students that authors write for different purposes. Suggested language: "Authors can write to entertain, to inform, or to persuade. Thinking about what kind of writing a book is and what the author wants you to gain from reading it can help you explain the author's purpose. What is the author's purpose for writing this biography?" (*to inform readers about Mandela's life*) Follow-up: "How do you know?" (*Biographies give information about someone's life, and this biography tells about Nelson Mandela.*)

SUMMARIZE AND APPLY Restate the minilesson principle. Tell students to apply it to their independent reading. Suggested language: "When you read, think about the genre of the book and how it helps you explain the author's purpose for writing."

GROUP SHARE Ask students to name the genre of a book they read. Then have them explain the author's purpose for writing it.

▶ Langston Hughes: A Poet and a Dreamer

INTERACTIVE READ-ALOUD/SHARED READING

Read aloud the selection to students. Stop periodically for brief discussion of the text. Use the following suggested stopping points and prompts:

- After reading the introduction, say: "What have you learned about Langston Hughes?"
- After reading the first poem, ask: "What do you think this poem is about?" (*It's about how having dreams can change the world.*) Follow-up: "How does this poem connect to what you learned about Langston Hughes's life?"
- After reading the last poem, ask students to turn and tell a partner which poem they liked best and why. Have students explain what the poem means to them.

MINILESSON Genre: Poetry

TEACH Display the minilesson principle on chart paper, and read it aloud to students. Explain that they are going to look back at *Langston Hughes* to learn to notice the words a poet uses to show how he feels about the topic.

1. Explain to students that words can make them feel a certain way. Ask students to volunteer words that make them feel excited, nervous, and sad. Then tell them that poets choose words carefully to help readers understand precisely how they feel about a topic.

> **MINILESSON PRINCIPLE**
>
> Readers notice how poets use words in unique ways to express feeling.

2. Reread the poem "Dreams" aloud to students. Then focus on the words in the first stanza. Suggested language: "Let's look at the first part of the poem. The poet says that life without dreams is like a bird that cannot fly. How do you think he feels about dreams?"

3. Next, discuss the second stanza. Point out the phrase *barren field,* and discuss the literal meaning with students. Then ask: "How would looking at a barren field make you feel?" Follow-up: "The poet says that without dreams, life is like a barren field. Why do you think he chose these words to show how he feels about dreams?"

SUMMARIZE AND APPLY Restate the minilesson principle. Tell students to apply it to their independent reading. Suggested language: "When you read a poem, look for the ways the poet uses words in unique ways to express their feelings."

GROUP SHARE Ask students to share a poem with others and to talk about how the poet used words to express feelings.

Whole-Group Lessons • 43

Whole-Group Lessons

How Tía Lola Came to Stay
Student Book, Lesson 3

Hannah in California
Teacher's Edition, Lesson 3

Pizza Pizzazz
Student Book, Lesson 3

▶ How Tía Lola Came to Stay

INTERACTIVE READ-ALOUD/SHARED READING

Read aloud the story to students. Stop periodically for very brief discussion of the text. Use the following suggested stopping points and prompts for quick group response, or give a specific prompt and have partners or threes turn and talk.

- After reading the introduction, ask: "Where does this story take place?" (*Vermont*) Follow-up: "How do you think Vermont is different from New York City and from the Dominican Republic?"
- After Miguel gets his Great Idea, ask: "What problem does Miguel have?" (*He has made his aunt feel bad.*) Follow-up: "Turn and talk with a partner about how Miguel might solve his problem."
- At the end of the story, ask: "What kind of person is Miguel? Turn and talk about your thinking with a partner."

MINILESSON Cause and Effect

TEACH Display the minilesson principle on chart paper, and read it aloud to students. Explain that a cause is an action or event that makes something else happen. An effect is the event that happens as a result of the cause. Tell students that they are going to talk about how some events in *How Tía Lola Came to Stay* cause other events to happen.

1. Use an event from the story to demonstrate cause-and-effect relationships. Suggested language: "Miguel decided to do something special for Tía Lola because he made her feel bad. Making Tía Lola feel bad was a cause. The effect was that Miguel wanted to do something special for her." Tell students that noticing causes and effects will help them understand why characters do or say certain things.

> **MINILESSON PRINCIPLE**
>
> Readers notice how events in a story cause other events to happen.

2. Focus on another event in the story, such as when Tía Lola felt better at the end of the story. Suggested language: "Why did Tía Lola feel better at the end of the story? What was the cause?"

3. Work with students to name other causes and effects in the story. Record students' ideas in a T-Map like the one shown here.

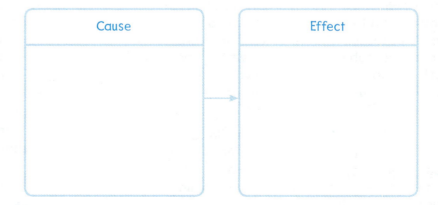

SUMMARIZE AND APPLY Restate the minilesson principle. Then tell students to apply it to their independent reading. Suggested language: "When you read a story, think about the events that cause other events to happen."

GROUP SHARE Ask students name a cause and an effect in the story they read. Have them explain how noticing causes and effects helps them understand the story.

Lesson 3

▶ Hannah in California

INTERACTIVE READ-ALOUD/SHARED READING

Read aloud the story to students. Stop periodically for brief discussion of the text. Use the following suggested stopping points and prompts:

- After Hannah sees the welcome sign, ask: "How would you feel if you received a welcome to a new place like Hannah did?"
- After reading that Hannah is homesick, say: "Mrs. Moore has noticed something about Hannah. Turn and talk with a partner about how you think Mrs. Moore will help her."
- At the end of the story, ask: "How do you think Mrs. Moore succeeded in helping Hannah?"

MINILESSON Cause and Effect

TEACH Write the minilesson principle on chart paper, and discuss it with students. Remind students that events can cause other events to happen. Explain that events can also affect characters and how they feel. Tell students that they will look at how events affect characters' feelings in *Hannah in California*.

1. Focus on the fact that Hannah felt homesick after she arrived at her new home. Suggested language: "Hannah felt homesick and alone after she came to an unfamiliar place. What are some events or causes for Hannah feeling homesick?"

> **MINILESSON PRINCIPLE**
>
> Readers notice how events affect characters and their feelings.

2. Remind students that Hannah's feelings at the end of the story changed. Ask students to explain the events that caused Hannah to feel more positive about California.

3. Then discuss Mrs. Moore with students. Work with them to identify events that changed how she felt. Record students' responses on a T-Map labeled *Cause* and *Effect*.

SUMMARIZE AND APPLY Restate the minilesson principle. Tell students to apply it to their independent reading. Suggested language: "When you read, think about how the events affect characters and their feelings. Noticing the causes for characters' feelings will help you understand them and what makes them happy or sad."

GROUP SHARE Ask students to tell how the characters feel in a story they read. Have them tell what events made them feel that way.

▶ Pizza Pizzazz

INTERACTIVE READ-ALOUD/SHARED READING

Read aloud the selection to students. Stop periodically for brief discussion of the text. Use the following suggested stopping points and prompts:

- After reading the introduction, ask: "What have you learned about pizza that you didn't know before?"
- After reading the section Pizza Dominicana, ask: "Why does the author put the list of ingredients in a special box at the beginning of the recipe?" (*so you know what you need before you start to make the pizza*)
- After reading the selection, ask students to turn and talk with a partner about whether making a pizza is easier or harder than they thought before reading the recipes.

MINILESSON Directions

TEACH Display the minilesson principle on chart paper, and read it aloud to students. Explain that together you are going to look back at *Pizza Pizzazz* to notice how the author helps them understand how to make pizza.

1. Guide students to describe the parts of the Pizza Dominicana recipe, including the tips, ingredients, numbered steps, and ending. Then ask: "Which parts of the recipe are most important to making a good pizza?" (*ingredients and numbered steps*) Follow-up: "What could happen if you didn't follow the order of steps that the recipe gives?"

> **MINILESSON PRINCIPLE**
>
> Readers notice how authors present information to explain a process.

2. Tell students that when an author presents information as steps, the steps are important to doing a task correctly. Have students turn the page and look at the next recipe. Ask them to turn and talk with a partner about how to design their own pizza.

SUMMARIZE AND APPLY Restate the minilesson principle. Tell students to apply it to their independent reading. Suggested language: "When you read directions for how to make something, look for the way the author presents information to explain the process."

GROUP SHARE Ask students to explain something they learned how to do from reading steps in a process. Remind them to tell the important steps in order.

Whole-Group Lessons • 45

Whole-Group Lessons

The Power of W.O.W.!
Student Book, Lesson 4

Bookmobile Rescue
Teacher's Edition, Lesson 4

Knowing Noses: Search-and-Rescue Dogs
Student Book, Lesson 4

▶ The Power of W.O.W.!

INTERACTIVE READ-ALOUD/SHARED READING

Read aloud the play to students. Stop periodically for very brief discussion. Use the following suggested stopping points and prompts for quick group response, or give a specific prompt and have partners or threes turn and talk.

- After reading Act One, Scene One, ask: "What problem do the characters have?" (*They don't have money to keep the bookmobile running.*)
- After reading Act One, Scene Two, say: "It sounds like these friends are devising a plan to save W.O.W. Why do you think they ask for Jake's advice?" (*He is Shane's older brother, and he helped to raise money for a class trip. He has some experience.*)
- After Ileana gets Mr. Diaz to agree to have the car wash, ask: "How would you describe Ileana? Turn and talk with a partner about your thinking."
- At the end of the play, ask: "How do Ileana and the others solve the problem?" (*They have a car wash that raises money for W.O.W., and the news attention of their car wash brought in donations as well.*)

MINILESSON Theme

TEACH Display the minilesson principle on chart paper, and read it aloud to students. Explain to students that authors may write a story to share a message or a lesson about life. Tell students that they are going to think about how they can look at the characters' actions to understand the lesson about life that the author was trying to teach. Explain that the message is called the story's theme.

1. Guide students as they discuss what Ileana and the others did in *The Power of W.O.W.!* Suggested language: "When Ileana discovered that the bookmobile was going to stop running, she met with others to talk about what they could do to save it. What plan did they make?"

2. Discuss the theme of the play with students. Suggested language: "Think about how many people in the community helped to save the bookmobile. How were each of their actions important?" (*Everyone who contributed something played an important role—the children who organized it, Mr. Diaz's donation of the water and parking lot, and the people who mailed in money.*) Follow-up: "What lesson did the characters' actions teach you?" (*People working together can accomplish more than one person can accomplish alone.*)

3. Have students recall another story they have read. Guide them to explain the lesson about life that they learned from the characters' actions.

> **MINILESSON PRINCIPLE**
>
> Readers think about how the characters' actions teach a lesson about life.

SUMMARIZE AND APPLY Restate the minilesson principle. Then tell students to apply it to their independent reading. Suggested language: "When you read a story or play, think about how the characters' actions teach you a lesson about life."

GROUP SHARE Ask students to share some lessons they learned in stories and plays they read.

46 • Lesson 4

Lesson 4

▶ Bookmobile Rescue

INTERACTIVE READ-ALOUD/SHARED READING

Read aloud the story to students. Stop periodically for brief discussion of the text. Use the following suggested stopping points and prompts:

- After Jessica and Alex talk, ask: "What problem does Alex have?" (*He needs to find a computer to write a report.*)
- After reading about Aunt Clara's idea, ask: "Why do you think that Aunt Clara's solution will work? Turn and talk with a partner about your thinking."
- At the end of the story, ask: "How do Jessica and Alex feel about Aunt Clara?" Follow-up: "What makes you think they feel that way?"

MINILESSON Genre: Realistic Fiction

TEACH Tell students that knowing what different kinds of stories are like will help them understand what happens and what to expect as they read. Tell students that realistic fiction is one kind of story. Display the minilesson principle on chart paper, and read it aloud. Then use *Bookmobile Rescue* to discuss the genre characteristics of realistic fiction.

1. Focus on one event in the story, such as the discussion that Jessica and Alex had. Help students understand that this event could really happen in today's world. Suggested language: "Jessica and Alex seem just like people that I know. Why do you think their discussion seemed like one that two friends could really have in today's world?" (*They talked like kids today. They had a problem that kept them from writing a report, which is a problem that I could have.*)

> **MINILESSON PRINCIPLE**
>
> Readers think about how the events in realistic fiction could really happen in today's world.

2. Guide students to identify other events in the story that could happen in today's world. Have them describe how the story's events make the story seem realistic.

SUMMARIZE AND APPLY Restate the minilesson principle. Tell students to apply it to their independent reading. Suggested language: "When you read a story, think about whether the events could really happen in today's world."

GROUP SHARE Ask students to tell whether the story they read was realistic fiction. Have them point out events that could or could not happen in today's world.

▶ Knowing Noses

INTERACTIVE READ-ALOUD/SHARED READING

Read aloud the selection to students. Stop periodically for brief discussion of the text. Use the following suggested stopping points and prompts:

- After reading the section Noses to the Rescue!, ask: "Why are SAR dogs so useful?" (*They can smell better than people do, and they can follow scents underwater, on the ground, and in the air.*)
- After reading the section Qualities of a Good SAR Dog, ask: "What qualities does a SAR dog need to have?" Follow-up: "Turn and talk with a partner about which quality you think is most important."
- After reading the special feature, ask: "How is this section different from everything else in this selection?" (*This is a story about one SAR dog that saved a Boy Scout. The rest of the selection is about how SAR dogs are trained and how they work.*)

MINILESSON Genre: Informational Text

TEACH Display the minilesson principle on chart paper, and read it aloud to students. Explain to students that they are going to learn to use special features that will help them locate information in informational text.

1. Point out and read aloud the headings in *Knowing Noses*. Tell students that headings usually tell what a section is about, and they help to organize the author's ideas.

> **MINILESSON PRINCIPLE**
>
> Readers look for the features of informational text to locate information.

2. Write the selection's four headings on chart paper. Work with students to list the kinds of information in each section. Help them recognize that the heading relates to the information that follows it.

3. Explain to students that they can use headings to find information. Guide students to understand how headings help readers locate information. Suggested language: "Look at the headings. In which section would you look to find information about what kind of dog would be good for this job?" Repeat for the other sections.

SUMMARIZE AND APPLY Restate the minilesson principle. Tell students to apply it to their independent reading. Suggested language: "When you read informational text, read the headings. They can help you know where different kinds of information is located."

GROUP SHARE Ask students to share informational texts they read. Have them read several headings and briefly describe the kinds of information they read about after each one.

Whole-Group Lessons • 47

Whole-Group Lessons

Stormalong
Student Book, Lesson 5

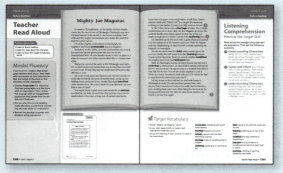

Mighty Joe Magarac
Teacher's Edition, Lesson 5

Hoderi the Fisherman
Student Book, Lesson 5

▶ Stormalong

INTERACTIVE READ-ALOUD/SHARED READING

Read aloud the story to students. Stop periodically for very brief discussion of the text. Use the following suggested stopping points and prompts for quick group response, or give a specific prompt and have partners or threes turn and talk.

- After the villagers name the giant baby Stormy, ask: "How do you know this is not a realistic story?" (*The baby is eighteen feet tall, and he drinks barrels of milk.*)
- After Stormy meets the captain in Boston Harbor, ask: "What problem does Stormy have?" (*He is too big to live in town.*) Follow-up: "How does he plan to solve it?"
- After Stormy returns to Boston because he yearns for the sea, say: "The author describes Stormy's condition after he returns to Boston. Why are the sailors surprised when they see him?" (*He doesn't look the same. He looks tired and worn.*)
- At the end of the story, ask: "How do the other sailors feel about Stormy?" Follow-up: "How do they show that they like him?"

MINILESSON Understanding Characters

TEACH Display the minilesson principle on chart paper, and read it aloud to students. Tell students that they are going to learn how details in a story will help them imagine and understand the main character.

1. Discuss the main character of *Stormalong* with students. Suggested language: "This story was about a giant sailor named Stormy. The author shared details that helped you imagine and understand what Stormy was like. What details helped you imagine the way he looked and sounded?" (*He was 18 feet tall; he cried as loud as a foghorn; ten people patted his back.*)

2. Point out that the author also gave readers details about how Stormy felt and why he did certain things. Suggested language: "How did Stormy feel when he left Cape Cod? What details did the author tell you to help you understand?"

3. Page through the story with students to locate more details about Stormy that paint a picture of him in readers' minds. Work with students to record details about Stormy in a Web like the one shown here.

> **MINILESSON PRINCIPLE**
> Readers look for details to help them imagine and understand the main character.

SUMMARIZE AND APPLY Restate the minilesson principle. Then tell students to apply it to their independent reading. Suggested language: "When you read a story, think about the details the author includes to help you imagine and understand the main character."

GROUP SHARE Ask students to name the main characters in a story they read. Have them share details that helped them imagine and understand the character.

Lesson 5

▶ Mighty Joe Magarac

INTERACTIVE READ-ALOUD/SHARED READING

Read aloud the story to students. Stop periodically for brief discussion of the text. Use the following suggested stopping points and prompts:

- After reading that Joe was made of steel, ask: "How does the author help you imagine young Joe and where he lives?"
- After reading about how Joe built a new fleet, ask: "In what other ways could Joe have helped people? Turn and talk with a partner about your thinking."
- At the end of the story, ask: "How is Joe like a real man?" Follow-up: "How is Joe not like a real man?"

MINILESSON Understanding Characters

TEACH Display the minilesson principle on chart paper, and read it aloud to students. Explain to students that thinking about what characters are like can help them predict what characters will do in stories such as *Mighty Joe Magarac*.

1. Discuss Joe's characteristics with students. Suggested language: "In the story you learned what Joe looked like. You also learned about the kind of man he was. What are some words that describe what Joe was like?" (*strong, helpful, hardworking, unselfish, successful*)

> **MINILESSON PRINCIPLE**
>
> Readers think about what characters are like to predict what they will do next.

2. Point out to students that when Joe first reported for work, he worked longer and harder than anyone else. He also did things that no one else could do.
3. Connect this information to making predictions about what Joe will do. Suggested language: "At the beginning of the story, Joe could do no wrong. He completed and succeeded at every task he was given. Knowing this information about Joe, what did you expect to happen when you read about the shortage of ships in the 1940s?"
4. Guide students to explain other predictions they could make about Joe based on his characteristics at the beginning of the story and at the end.

SUMMARIZE AND APPLY Restate the minilesson principle. Tell students to apply it to their independent reading. Suggested language: "When you read a story, think about what the characters are like to help you predict what they might do."

GROUP SHARE Ask students to describe some characters in a story they read. Have them tell how knowing what these characters were like helped them to predict what they did in the story.

▶ Hoderi the Fisherman

INTERACTIVE READ-ALOUD/SHARED READING

Read aloud the play to students. Stop periodically for brief discussion of the text. Use the following suggested stopping points and prompts:

- After reading the first page, ask: "What information does the author include on the first page?" (*the play's title, the characters' names and how to say them, the play's setting—where and when it takes place*)
- After reading the second page, ask: "What kind of information does the narrator tell you in this play?" (*The narrator gives information that isn't included in the dialogue, such as what the characters do.*)
- At the end of the play, ask: "How might the play have ended if Katsumi listened to her father? Turn and talk with a partner about your thinking."

MINILESSON Genre: Play

TEACH Display the minilesson principle on chart paper, and read it aloud to students. Explain that stage directions are parts of a play that are not read aloud. They tell the actors what to do, and they explain how to set up the stage for a performance. Tell students that they are going to look at the stage directions in *Hoderi the Fisherman* to help them understand the setting and action.

1. Focus on one stage direction in Scene One, such as *[Hoderi dives into the water.]*. Suggested language: "This stage direction tells you what a character is doing. If you were watching a performance of the play, the actor playing Hoderi would dive into water."

> **MINILESSON PRINCIPLE**
>
> Readers notice stage directions in a play to understand the setting and action.

2. Point out to students that stage directions often explain how a line should be read and the emotion that the character should have. Have students point out stage directions in this play that explain emotion.
3. Draw students' attention to stage directions that describe setting and discuss them.

SUMMARIZE AND APPLY Restate the minilesson principle. Tell students to apply it to their independent reading. Suggested language: "When you read a play, use the stage directions to understand the action and setting."

GROUP SHARE Ask students to share a stage direction from a play they read. Have them tell how it helped them understand something about the play.

Whole-Group Lessons • 49

Whole-Group Lessons

Once Upon a Cool Motorcycle Dude
Student Book, Lesson 6

Tim Wishes Twice
Teacher's Edition, Lesson 6

Storyteller Diane Ferlatte
Student Book, Lesson 6

▶ **Once Upon a Cool Motorcycle Dude**

INTERACTIVE READ-ALOUD/SHARED READING

Read aloud the story to students. Stop periodically for very brief discussion of the text. Use the following suggested stopping points and prompts for quick group response, or give a specific prompt and have partners or threes turn and talk.

- After reading the first two pages of the story, ask: "Who is telling this story?" Follow-up: "What can you tell about how they want to tell the story?" *(They have different ideas about the story. They both think their version is better.)*
- After the giant takes away all the ponies except Buttercup, ask: "What do you think the princess will do now? Turn and talk about your thinking with a partner."
- After the giant steals the last pony, ask: "How does the story change when the boy starts telling his part?" Follow-up: "What is different about the illustrations?"
- After Princess Tenderheart becomes Princess Warrior, ask: "How is Princess Warrior different from Princess Tenderheart?"
- At the end of the story, ask: "How do the boy and girl feel about their story now? Why do you think so?"

MINILESSON Compare and Contrast

TEACH Display the minilesson principle on chart paper, and read it aloud to students. Tell students that comparing and contrasting characters can help them better understand what the characters are like.

1. Discuss the principle with students, using examples of characters from *Once Upon a Cool Motorcycle Dude*. Suggested language: "You read about a boy and girl who wrote a fairy tale together. How did they feel about each other's ideas for the story?" Follow-up: "What did they say and do to let you know they felt that way?"

2. Explain to students that what the characters say and do are clues to what they are like. Suggested language: "The boy and girl interrupted each other when they told the story. They gave their own ideas about what should happen next. What did their ideas about what should happen next in the story tell you about what the two characters were like?"

3. Elicit from students examples from the story that showed how the boy and girl were alike and different. Record students' ideas in a Venn Diagram like the one shown here.

> **MINILESSON PRINCIPLE**
> Readers compare and contrast characters to understand how they are alike and different.

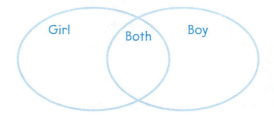

SUMMARIZE AND APPLY Restate the minilesson principle. Then tell students to apply it to their independent reading. Suggested language: "When you read, think about what the characters say and do. Think about how the characters are alike and different."

GROUP SHARE Ask students to tell about two characters in a story they read. Have them explain how the characters are alike and different.

50 • Lesson 6

Lesson 6

▶ Tim Wishes Twice

INTERACTIVE READ-ALOUD/SHARED READING

Read aloud the story to students. Stop periodically for brief discussion of the text. Use the following suggested stopping points and prompts:

- After Tim gets angry at his brother, ask: "What kind of day is Tim having so far?" Follow-up: "Do you think it will get better? Why or why not?"
- After Tim tells Maria he forgot to bring in a picture for their project, ask: "How does Maria feel about the school project?" Follow-up: "Does Tim feel the same way? Why do you think so?"
- At the end of the story, ask: "How is Tim's attitude at the beginning of the story different from his attitude at the end of the story? Turn and talk about your thinking with a partner."

MINILESSON Understanding Characters

TEACH Display the minilesson principle on chart paper, and read it aloud to students. Tell students they are going to learn about how the choices characters make can help them learn what they are like.

1. Talk with students about the motivation for Tim's first wish in *Tim Wishes Twice*. Suggested language: "Tim wished he wouldn't be able to hear people talking to him. Why do you think Tim made that wish?" *(He felt that he was having a bad day, and he didn't want to hear others criticize him for forgetting about the school project.)*

> **MINILESSON PRINCIPLE**
>
> Readers think about characters' choices and what their choices tell you about them.

2. Point out to students that Tim's wish showed he was not responsible. Suggested language: "Tim's action showed that he was careless with his wish. Tim didn't think about the consequences of what he asked for."

3. Next, focus on Tim's second wish. Suggested language: "Next, Tim wished he *could* hear people talk to him. Why did Tim want to change his first wish?" *(Not being able to hear people made him feel invisible.)* "What did this tell you about Tim? Turn and tell a partner what you thought about Tim by the end of the story."

SUMMARIZE AND APPLY Restate the minilesson principle. Tell students to apply it to their independent reading. Suggested language: "When you read, think about the choices characters make. Think about how those choices help you understand what the characters are like."

GROUP SHARE Ask students to share an example of something a character does in a story they read. Have them explain what they learned about the character by thinking about the choices he or she made.

▶ Storyteller Diane Ferlatte

INTERACTIVE READ-ALOUD/SHARED READING

Read aloud the selection to students. Stop periodically for brief discussion of the text. Use the following suggested stopping points and prompts:

- After reading the introduction, ask: "How does the author get your attention at the beginning of this selection?" *(She uses questions to help readers think about the idea of storytelling.)*
- After reading the section Childhood Memories, ask: "Why does the author talk about Diane Ferlatte's childhood?" *(It helps you understand why Diane Ferlatte became a storyteller.)*
- At the end of the selection, ask: "What do the photos and quotes tell you about Diane Ferlatte? Turn and talk about your ideas with a partner."

MINILESSON Genre: Informational Text

TEACH Display the minilesson principle on chart paper, and read it aloud to students. Tell students that they are going to learn about how the details in a selection can help them understand the author's attitude toward the subject, or how she feels about it.

1. Discuss examples in *Storyteller Diane Ferlatte* that help students understand how the author feels about Diane Ferlatte and storytelling. Suggested language: "In the selection, the author told about the many times Diane Ferlatte spent listening to other family members tell stories. How can you tell that the author agrees with Diane Ferlatte that storytelling is an important tradition?" *(The details that the author chose to include about Diane Ferlatte's childhood show that stories brought her a lot of joy as a child.)*

> **MINILESSON PRINCIPLE**
>
> Readers notice details to understand the author's attitude toward the subject.

2. Work with students to identify other details in the selection that are clues to how the author feels about storytelling. Point out the author's choice of quotes and photos to highlight what she felt was important. Write students' ideas in a T-Map labeled *Detail* and *What It Shows*.

SUMMARIZE AND APPLY Restate the minilesson principle. Tell students that when they read, they should look for details that help them understand the author's attitude toward the subject. Suggested language: "When you read, look for details that tell how the author feels about the subject."

GROUP SHARE Ask students to share important details in a selection they read. Have them tell how the details helped them understand the author's attitude toward the subject.

Whole-Group Lessons • 51

Whole-Group Lessons

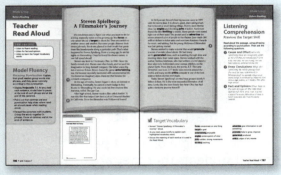

Coming Distractions: Questioning Movies
Student Book, Lesson 7

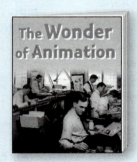

Steven Spielberg: A Filmmaker's Journey
Teacher's Edition, Lesson 7

The Wonder of Animation
Student Book, Lesson 7

▶ Coming Distractions: Questioning Movies

INTERACTIVE READ-ALOUD/SHARED READING

Read aloud the selection to students. Stop periodically for very brief discussion of the text. Use the following suggested stopping points and prompts for quick group response, or give a specific prompt and have partners or threes turn and talk.

- After reading the section Painting a "Bad" Picture, ask: "What is the author saying about the choices that moviemakers make?" *(They sometimes leave things out of a movie to keep the movie interesting and so that viewers don't get bored.)*
- After reading the section How Does the Message Get My Attention?, ask: "How do movie studios advertise?" Follow-up: "Which technique do you think is best to get the attention of people your age? Turn and talk about your ideas with a partner."
- After reading the section Jolts Per Minute, say: "The author tells about some of the ingredients that make movies fun. Turn and talk with a partner about how some of these ingredients were used in your favorite movies."

MINILESSON Fact and Opinion

TEACH Display the minilesson principle on chart paper, and read it aloud to students. Explain that facts are statements that can be proved. Opinions are someone's thoughts, feelings, or beliefs about something. Tell students that it is important to notice the difference between facts and opinions as they read because they can agree or disagree with opinions.

1. Discuss the principle, using examples from *Coming Distractions: Questioning Movies*. Suggested language: "The author said that *a leading man doesn't look as good driving a rusty old car*. Is this a fact or an opinion?" *(opinion)* "How do you know?" *(The idea can't be proved by checking in a reference book or another reliable source.)*
2. Reread the section Mixing Up a Movie with students. Guide them to name a fact or an opinion and tell how they know.
3. Explain to students that some words and phrases are clues that the author is stating an opinion. Write the following examples on chart paper: *should, best, I think, believe*.
4. Elicit from students additional examples of facts and opinions in the selection. Record students' ideas in a T-Map like the one shown here. Have volunteers tell whether they agree with the opinions and why.

> **MINILESSON PRINCIPLE**
>
> Readers notice the difference between facts and the author's thoughts, feelings, or beliefs.

Fact	Opinion

SUMMARIZE AND APPLY Restate the minilesson principle. Then tell students to apply it to their independent reading. Suggested language: "When you read, look for facts and what the author thinks, feels, or believes. Think about how you know the difference between facts and opinions."

GROUP SHARE Ask students to share a fact and an opinion they found in their reading. Tell them to explain how they knew it was a fact or an opinion.

Lesson 7

▶ Steven Spielberg: A Filmmaker's Journey

INTERACTIVE READ-ALOUD/SHARED READING

Read aloud the selection to students. Stop periodically for brief discussion of the text. Use the following suggested stopping points and prompts:

- After reading the first paragraph, ask: "Why does the author explain that some people discover their dream job early in life and some do not?" *(to emphasize that Steven Spielberg was destined to be a filmmaker from a young age)*
- After reading the second paragraph, ask: "What was Steven Spielberg's life like when he was young?" *(He moved a lot and was often lonely.)* Follow-up: "How do you think this affected the kinds of films he makes? Turn and talk about your thinking with a partner."
- At the end of the selection, ask: "Why do you think the author wrote this selection?"

MINILESSON Fact and Opinion

TEACH Display the minilesson principle on chart paper, and read it aloud to students. Tell students they are going to learn about how to recognize the difference between facts and opinions. Remind them that facts can be proved and opinions tell a person's thoughts, feelings, or beliefs about something.

1. Discuss the principle with students, using examples from *Steven Spielberg*. Suggested language: "The author says that Steven Spielberg is the most successful filmmaker of all time. Think about whether this statement can be proved. Is it a fact or an opinion?" *(fact)* "How do you know?" *(The author says that his movies have earned nearly 8 billion dollars.)*

> **MINILESSON PRINCIPLE**
>
> Readers recognize that facts can be proved and that opinions cannot be proved.

2. Read aloud a mixture of facts and opinions from the selection as you record them in a T-Map on chart paper. Ask students to explain whether they are facts or opinions.

3. Encourage students to explain how the facts can be proved and whether they agree with the opinions.

SUMMARIZE AND APPLY Restate the minilesson principle. Tell students to apply it to their independent reading. Suggested language: "When you read, think about the ideas in the selection and whether they are facts that can be proved or opinions."

GROUP SHARE Ask students to share a statement from a selection they read. Have them tell whether it is a fact or an opinion.

▶ The Wonder of Animation

INTERACTIVE READ-ALOUD/SHARED READING

Read aloud the selection to students. Stop periodically for brief discussion of the text. Use the following suggested stopping points and prompts:

- After reading the introduction, ask: "How does the author probably feel about animation?" Follow-up: "What clues does she use to show her feelings?"
- After reading the section Animation Grows Up, ask: "How have animated films changed over time?" *(They look more realistic; animation can be created with computers; animation is advertised for all ages.)*
- At the end of the selection, ask: "What are some reasons that people enjoy animation? Turn and talk about your thinking with a partner."

MINILESSON Genre: Informational Text

TEACH Display the minilesson principle on chart paper, and read it aloud to students. Tell students that they are going to learn about how the features of an informational text can help them understand the topic better.

1. Discuss the principle with students, using examples from *The Wonder of Animation*. Suggested language: "The author used special features to help you understand different things about the topic of animation. What were these features?" *(photos, captions, headings, timeline, sidebar)*

> **MINILESSON PRINCIPLE**
>
> Readers use the features of informational text to help them understand the topic.

2. Draw students' attention to the headings. Ask: "What did the headings tell you?" *(They were clues to what each section was about.)* Follow-up: "Where would you read to learn about the first animated films?"

3. Next, focus on the timeline. Explain that the author used a timeline to tell about when important events in the history of animated films occurred. Review the timeline with students, and discuss why each event was important. Point out that the timeline gave information that was not included in the main part of the selection.

4. Have students explain the importance of the other features.

SUMMARIZE AND APPLY Restate the minilesson principle. Tell students to apply it to their independent reading. Suggested language: "When you read, think about features the author used and what those features helped you understand about the topic."

GROUP SHARE Ask students to share what they learned from a feature in a selection they read. Have them explain how the feature helped them understand more about the topic.

Whole-Group Lessons • 53

Whole-Group Lessons

Me and Uncle Romie
Student Book, Lesson 8

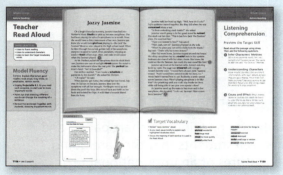

Jazzy Jasmine
Teacher's Edition, Lesson 8

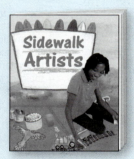

Sidewalk Artists
Student Book, Lesson 8

▶ Me and Uncle Romie

INTERACTIVE READ-ALOUD/SHARED READING

Read aloud the story to students. Stop periodically for very brief discussion of the text. Use the following suggested stopping points and prompts for quick group response, or give a specific prompt and have partners or threes turn and talk.

- After James and Aunt Nanette climb the stairs to the apartment, ask: "Who is telling this story?" Follow-up: "Where does the story take place?"
- After Aunt Nanette tells James she has to go away, ask: "Why doesn't James want his Aunt Nanette to leave? Turn and talk about your thinking with a partner."
- After Aunt Nanette returns home, ask: "How do James's feelings about Uncle Romie change after he spends time with him?" *(He realizes Uncle Romie is a good man and that they have a lot in common.)*
- Focus on the picture at the end of the selection. Ask: "What does James do at the end of the story?" Follow-up: "How does he make his collage special for Uncle Romie?"

MINILESSON Understanding Characters

TEACH Display the minilesson principle on chart paper, and read it aloud to students. Explain that authors use different clues to help readers get to know characters and understand what they are like.

1. Discuss the principle, using examples from *Me and Uncle Romie*. Suggested language: "At the beginning of the story, the author started including clues to help you understand Uncle Romie. Aunt Nanette said he's preparing for a big art show and working hard. She also said he's a collage artist. One way to learn about characters is by reading what others characters say about them."

2. Ask students to think about Uncle Romie once he and James spent time together. Suggested language: "Another way to get to know characters is by what they say and do. What did you learn about Uncle Romie when he spent time with James?" *(He was caring because he made James's birthday special. He was also mischievous because he said he snuck pepper jelly when Grandma wasn't looking.)*

3. Elicit from students additional clues showing what characters in the story were like. Record students' ideas in a T-Map like the one shown here.

> **MINILESSON PRINCIPLE**
>
> Readers notice the ways in which the author helps them get to know the characters.

Clue	What We Learn About the Character

SUMMARIZE AND APPLY Restate the minilesson principle. Then tell students to apply it to their independent reading. Suggested language: "When you read, think about what the characters say and do. Notice what other characters say about them. These clues will help you get to know the characters."

GROUP SHARE Ask students to share what they learned about one character in a story they read. Have them explain clues that helped them know what that character was like.

54 • Lesson 8

Lesson 8

▶ Jazzy Jasmine

INTERACTIVE READ-ALOUD/SHARED READING

Read aloud the story to students. Stop periodically for brief discussion of the text. Use the following suggested stopping points and prompts:

- After reading the first page, ask: "What kind of person is Jasmine?" Follow-up: "How do you know?"
- After Saji asks Jasmine if she has *listened* to Jack the Saxman, say: "Saji doesn't seem to be impressed with Jasmine's playing. What is she trying to tell Jasmine?" *(Playing the saxophone is more about how you sound than how you look.)*
- At the end of the selection, ask: "What does Jasmine learn in this story? Turn and talk about your thinking with a partner."

MINILESSON Understanding Characters

TEACH Display the minilesson principle on chart paper, and read it aloud to students. Tell students that they will learn how a character in *Jazzy Jasmine* is influenced by others.

1. Talk with students about Jasmine's reason for wanting a saxophone. Suggested language: "Jasmine wanted to look like Jack the Saxman when she played. Watching him play influenced Jasmine to want her own shiny instrument to play."

> **MINILESSON PRINCIPLE**
>
> Readers notice how characters influence one another to understand what they do and how they feel.

2. Then tell students that characters can change how other characters feel. Have students explain how Jasmine felt after playing for Saji. Suggested language: "Saji told Jasmine that Jack the Saxman moved around because he felt the music and not to look good. How did Jasmine feel right after talking to Saji?" *(She was upset because she didn't think she could ever sound like Jack the Saxman.)*

3. Remind students that Jasmine was happier by the end of the story. Work with them to explain what changed for Jasmine and who influenced her to change what she did and how she felt.

SUMMARIZE AND APPLY Restate the minilesson principle. Tell students to apply it to their independent reading. Suggested language: "When you read, notice how characters influence one another. Think about how it helps you understand what the characters do and how they feel."

GROUP SHARE Ask students to share an example from a story they read of how one character influenced another to do something or feel a certain way. Have them tell what they learned about those characters.

▶ Sidewalk Artists

INTERACTIVE READ-ALOUD/SHARED READING

Read aloud the play to students. Stop periodically for brief discussion of the text. Use the following suggested stopping points and prompts:

- After reading the first page, ask: "What do you think you will learn from this selection?" *(how to do wet-chalk drawing)* Follow-up: "How do you know?" *(The students are preparing for an art show, and Ms. Lee is about to review the steps.)*
- At the end of the selection, ask: "What have the students discovered?" *(a new technique for making chalk drawings)* Follow-up: "How do the students feel about their new artwork? How do you know?"

MINILESSON Directions

TEACH Display the minilesson principle on chart paper, and read it aloud to students. Tell students that they are going to learn about ways that authors show steps for how to do something.

1. Discuss the principle with students, using examples from *Sidewalk Artists*. Suggested language: "In the selection, the author used two different ways to give instructions for how to create a wet-chalk drawing. What are these ways?" *(through dialogue and through numbered steps)* Follow-up: "What other ways could you show steps in a process? Turn and talk about your ideas with a partner."

> **MINILESSON PRINCIPLE**
>
> Readers notice how authors may show steps in a process in different ways.

2. Focus on the numbered steps at the end. Suggested language: "The author used a numbered list to show the steps for making a wet-chalk drawing. Why is a numbered list easier to use when you are following steps in a process?"

SUMMARIZE AND APPLY Restate the minilesson principle. Explain to students that they should notice how authors show steps in a process as they read. Suggested language: "When you read, notice how the author shows steps in a process. Think about how it helps you understand how to do something."

GROUP SHARE Ask students to share an example of steps in a process from a selection they read. Have them explain how it helped them understand the process.

Whole-Group Lessons • 55

Whole-Group Lessons

Dear Mr. Winston
Student Book, Lesson 9

Is Sasquatch Out There?
Teacher's Edition, Lesson 9

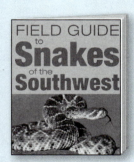

Field Guide to Snakes of the Southwest
Student Book, Lesson 9

▶ **Dear Mr. Winston**

INTERACTIVE READ-ALOUD/SHARED READING

Read aloud the story to students. Stop periodically for very brief discussion of the text. Use the following suggested stopping points and prompts for quick group response, or give a specific prompt and have partners or threes turn and talk.

- After reading the first page, ask: "How is this story different from most stories?" *(It is a letter.)* Follow-up: "Why do you think the author writes the story in the form of a letter?"
- After reading the second page, ask: "What do you think about the girl's apology so far? Turn and talk with a partner about whether you think it's sincere."
- After reading that Jake Lambert says the snake is perfectly harmless, ask: "What does the girl think of Mr. Winston's fear of snakes? What does the author say to make you think that?"
- At the end of the selection, ask: "What makes this story so funny? Turn and talk with a partner about your thinking."

MINILESSON Conclusions

TEACH Display the minilesson principle on chart paper, and read it aloud to students. Explain that authors gives clues in a story to help readers figure out things that are not stated. Tell students that when they figure out something that the author did not say, they have drawn a conclusion.

1. Discuss the principle, using examples from *Dear Mr. Winston*. Suggested language: "On the second page of the letter, the writer said that she wanted to remind Mr. Winston about something before he was taken away in an ambulance. What does it mean when an ambulance picks someone up?" Use students' responses to point out that the writer didn't say that Mr. Winston was hurt, but they figured it out because of what they already know about ambulances.

> **MINILESSON PRINCIPLE**
>
> Readers notice that they can use clues to figure out things the author does not tell them.

2. Guide students to draw conclusions about how Cara's parents felt about what she did in the library. Help students recognize clues that helped them figure out that they were very upset with Cara. *(They made her write an apology letter, they didn't allow her to watch her favorite show anymore, and they sent Mr. Winston flowers.)*
3. Next, explain to students that the author gave clues throughout the letter that showed how the writer really felt about Mr. Winston's reaction to the snake in the library. Guide students to identify clues that helped them understand how Cara felt.
4. Record students' ideas in a T-Map like the one shown here.

Cara's Feelings	Clues

SUMMARIZE AND APPLY Restate the minilesson principle. Then tell students to apply it to their independent reading. Suggested language: "When you read, notice clues that authors include to help you figure out things they don't tell you in their stories."

GROUP SHARE Ask students to explain something in a story they read that the author did not tell them, but they figured out using clues and what they already know. Then have students tell the clues that helped them figure it out.

Lesson 9

▶ Is Sasquatch Out There?

INTERACTIVE READ-ALOUD/SHARED READING

Read aloud the selection to students. Stop periodically for brief discussion of the text. Use the following suggested stopping points and prompts:

- After reading the first paragraph, ask: "How do you think the author feels about legends?" Follow-up: "How can you tell?"
- After reading the second paragraph, say: "The author compares legends to a game called Telephone. Turn and talk with a partner about how this comparison helps you understand how legends change."
- At the end of the selection, ask: "What do you think the author believes about whether Sasquatch exists?"

MINILESSON Conclusions

TEACH Display the minilesson principle on chart paper, and read it aloud to students. Tell students they are going to think about whether the ideas an author gives are believable.

1. Tell students that sometimes authors share facts and different people's ideas about something, and they allow readers to draw their own conclusions about them. Explain that forming an opinion about whether something is believable is a type of conclusion.

2. Recall with students that there is a debate as to whether Sasquatch really exists. Focus on the part of the selection that discusses how some scientists, including Jane Goodall, have claimed that they believe Sasquatch may be real. Ask: "Knowing that some scientists believe it possible, do you believe that it is possible that Sasquatch exists? What is your opinion?" Have students turn and talk with a partner about their thinking.

3. Discuss the other evidence people have used to convince others that Sasquatch exists. Have students tell whether they think the evidence is believable and how it affects their own opinions.

> **MINILESSON PRINCIPLE**
>
> Readers think about whether the ideas an author gives are believable to form their own opinions.

SUMMARIZE AND APPLY Restate the minilesson principle. Tell students to apply it to their independent reading. Suggested language: "When you read, think about whether the ideas the author gives are believable to help you form your own opinions."

GROUP SHARE Ask students to share an idea from a book they have read. Have them tell whether they think the idea is believable and explain why.

▶ Field Guide to Snakes of the Southwest

INTERACTIVE READ-ALOUD/SHARED READING

Read aloud the selection to students. Stop periodically for brief discussion of the text. Use the following suggested stopping points and prompts:

- After reading the first page, ask: "What evidence does the author give to support the idea that snakes are amazing?" Follow-up: "Why do you agree or disagree?"
- After reading the three display boxes, ask: "What kinds of information does the author tell you about each snake?"
- At the end of the selection, ask: "How do you think the author feels about snakes? Turn and talk with a partner about your thinking."

MINILESSON Genre: Informational Text

TEACH Display the minilesson principle on chart paper, and read it aloud to students. Tell students that they are going to learn about how information can be organized into categories to explain a topic.

1. Discuss the principle with students, using examples from *Field Guide to Snakes of the Southwest*. Suggested language: "In the selection, the author grouped information about snakes of the southwest into three categories, or sections. He told all about one snake and then he told all about the next snake. How does this kind of organization help you understand the information?"

> **MINILESSON PRINCIPLE**
>
> Readers notice that authors may organize information in categories to explain a topic.

2. Focus on one of the boxes, such as the box for Western Diamond-Backed Rattlesnake, and explain that this is one category of information. Ask students to explain the information in this category.

3. Then move to the next category, and ask students to explain the information in it. Elicit from students that the same kinds of information are presented in each category.

SUMMARIZE AND APPLY Restate the minilesson principle. Tell students to apply it to their independent reading. Suggested language: "When you read, notice how the author organizes information in categories. Think about how this helps you understand the topic."

GROUP SHARE Ask students to share how information is organized in a selection they read. Have them explain how it helped them understand the topic.

Whole-Group Lessons • **57**

Whole-Group Lessons

José! Born to Dance
Student Book, Lesson 10

Mexican Dove
Teacher's Edition, Lesson 10

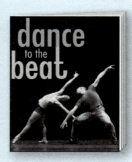

Dance to the Beat
Student Book, Lesson 10

▶ José! Born to Dance

INTERACTIVE READ-ALOUD/SHARED READING

Read aloud the selection to students. Stop periodically for very brief discussion of the text. Use the following suggested stopping points and prompts for quick group response, or give a specific prompt and have partners or threes turn and talk.

- After José's family leaves their home, ask: "Where did José live?" (*Mexico*) Follow-up: "What was it like in Mexico when José was young, and how did this affect his life?"
- After José gives up art, say: "The author uses the words *cemetery* and *jungle of stone* to describe how José felt about New York. How do these words make you feel about New York?"
- After reading about José's dancing, ask: "The author uses some words from earlier in the selection when describing José's dancing. Why do you think she does this?" (*to show how José used everything he learned in life in his dancing*)
- At the end of the selection, ask: "What does José's life teach you? Turn and talk about your thinking with a partner."

MINILESSON Genre: Biography

TEACH Display the minilesson principle on chart paper, and read it aloud to students. Remind students that biographies tell facts about a person's life. Explain that authors sometimes write biographies to show how a person overcomes hardships to succeed. Tell students that thinking about the hardships a person faced can help them understand what the person is like.

1. Discuss the principle, using examples from *José! Born to Dance*. Suggested language: "When José first went to school in the United States, he didn't know how to speak English. Why was this difficult for him?" (*He couldn't read or communicate, and others teased him.*) Follow-up: "How did José overcome this hardship?" (*He told himself that he would learn English better than any of his classmates, and within three years he was confident when he spoke English.*)

> **MINILESSON PRINCIPLE**
>
> Readers notice how the subject of a biography overcomes hardships to succeed.

2. Work with students to discuss other hardships José overcame in Mexico, California, and New York. Have students tell how he overcame each of these hardships.
3. Record students' ideas in a T-Map like the one shown here.

Hardship	How José Overcame It

SUMMARIZE AND APPLY Restate the minilesson principle. Then tell students to apply it to their independent reading. Suggested language: "When you read a biography, notice how the person you are reading about overcame hardships to succeed. Think about what it helps you learn about the person."

GROUP SHARE Ask students to share an example of a biography they read in which the person overcame a hardship to succeed.

58 • Lesson 10

Lesson 10

▶ Mexican Dove

INTERACTIVE READ-ALOUD/SHARED READING

Read aloud the biography to students. Stop periodically for brief discussion of the text. Use the following suggested stopping points and prompts:

- After reading the first paragraph, ask: "Who is this biography about?" *(Frida Kahlo)* Follow-up: "How does the author make you want to know more about Frida?"
- After reading about Frida's paintings, say: "Frida used the same vibrant colors and symbols that the native Mexicans used. What does that tell you about how she feels about Mexico?"
- At the end of the biography, ask: "How does Frida overcome her hardships? Turn and talk with a partner about how painting helped her."

MINILESSON Author's Purpose

TEACH Display the minilesson principle on chart paper, and read it aloud to students. Tell students that thinking about how an author feels about a subject can help them understand why the author wrote about that subject.

1. Discuss the principle, using examples from *Mexican Dove*. Focus on the first paragraph of the selection. Guide students to understand the author's feelings for Frida Kahlo. Suggested language: "How does the author feel about Frida?" Follow-up: "What words or phrases did the author use to let you know?" *("fragile and small," "stubborn interest," "shout her story")*

> **MINILESSON PRINCIPLE**
>
> Readers think about authors' feelings about their subject to understand why they wrote about it.

2. Reread the last paragraph aloud. Work with students to describe the author's feelings and to identify words or phrases that help them know. Guide students to recognize that the author thinks Frida's life story is important to share because her experiences may inspire other people to overcome problems.

3. Point out to students that authors often write biographies about subjects that they admire. Have students turn and talk with a partner about why authors would want to write about a person they admire.

SUMMARIZE AND APPLY Restate the minilesson principle. Tell students to apply it to their independent reading. Suggested language: "When you read, notice how the author feels about the subject. Think about how these feelings help you understand why the author wrote about the subject."

GROUP SHARE Ask students to share a selection they read. Have them tell how the author of the selection felt about the subject. Then ask them to tell how they knew.

▶ Dance to the Beat

INTERACTIVE READ-ALOUD/SHARED READING

Read aloud the poems to students. Stop periodically for brief discussion of the text. Use the following suggested stopping points and prompts:

- After reading the introduction, ask: "Why does the author compare poems to music and dance?"
- After reading "The Song of the Night," ask: "How does this poem make you feel about dancing? Turn and talk about your thinking with a partner."
- After reading the poem about Gene Kelly, ask: "Why does the author include a short biography of Gene Kelly?" *(If you don't know who Gene Kelly is, it helps you understand why the poet wrote a poem for him to dance to.)*

MINILESSON Genre: Poetry

TEACH Display the minilesson principle on chart paper, and read it aloud to students. Tell students that they are going to learn about how poets use the sound of words to create rhythm.

1. Explain to students that in poems rhythm is the beat of how the words are read. Like the beat of a song, a poem's rhythm can be fast or slow.

> **MINILESSON PRINCIPLE**
>
> Readers notice how poets use the sound of words to create rhythm.

2. Discuss the principle with students, using examples from "The Song of the Night." First, reread the poem, emphasizing the rhythm as you read. Then discuss the rhythm with students. Suggested language: "The poet used the sound of words to create a beat. She repeated the word *dance* to emphasize the beat. She also included rhyming words to create rhythm."

3. Focus on the other poems. Have students tell how the repeating words and rhyming words helped to create a rhythm. Ask students to read selected lines aloud to show the rhythm.

SUMMARIZE AND APPLY Restate the minilesson principle. Tell students to apply it to their independent reading. Suggested language: "When you read a poem, notice how the sound of the words helps create rhythm."

GROUP SHARE Ask students to share a poem they read. Have them point out how the sound of the words creates rhythm.

Whole-Group Lessons • 59

Whole-Group Lessons

The Screech Owl Who Liked Television
Student Book, Lesson 11

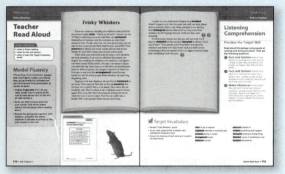

Frisky Whiskers
Teacher's Edition, Lesson 11

In the Wild
Student Book, Lesson 11

▶ **The Screech Owl Who Liked Television**

INTERACTIVE READ-ALOUD/SHARED READING

Read aloud the selection to students. Stop periodically for very brief discussion of the text. Use the following suggested stopping points and prompts for quick group response, or give a specific prompt and have partners or threes turn and talk.

- After reading the first page, ask: "What can you tell so far about the characters in this story?"
- After Twig gets permission to watch TV again, ask: "How would you describe the relationship between Twig and Yammer?" (*Twig treats Yammer like a person in the family.*)
- After reading about Yammer and the shower, say: "The author describes Yammer's interactions with this family in great detail. How does this affect the way you feel about Yammer?" (*You feel like you know Yammer.*)
- At the end of the story, ask: "How did the end of the story make you feel? Turn and talk with a partner about why you felt this way."

MINILESSON Genre: Narrative Nonfiction

TEACH Display the minilesson principle on chart paper, and read it aloud to students. Tell students that they are going to think about how narration and dialogue help them understand characters and events in a story.

1. Tell students that *The Screech Owl Who Liked Television* is a type of informational text called narrative nonfiction. Explain that the events in narrative nonfiction really happened, and the author explains the events in order like a story.

2. Point out to students that this story has a narrator who was part of the story. Suggested language: "The story was told by the mother of the family. She explained what happened in her own words."

3. Guide students to recognize that when a narrator is part of the story, readers find out what happened through that person's eyes. Ask students to explain what might be different about the story if it were told by Twig. Have them speculate about some different things they might have learned about the characters and events.

4. Next, point out that there is dialogue in the story shown in quotation marks. Suggested language: "Dialogue is what the characters in a story actually say. Because this story is true, the dialogue is the words that real people said, and it would not change if another person told the story."

5. Page through the selection with students, pointing out selected dialogue. Ask students to explain what they learned about the characters and events from the dialogue.

> **MINILESSON PRINCIPLE**
>
> Readers notice the difference between narration and dialogue to understand characters and events.

SUMMARIZE AND APPLY Restate the minilesson principle. Then tell students to apply it to their independent reading. Suggested language: "When you read a story, think about how the narration and the dialogue help you to understand the characters and events."

GROUP SHARE Ask students to explain the narration and dialogue in a story they read and share what they learned about the characters and events.

Lesson 11

▶ Frisky Whiskers

INTERACTIVE READ-ALOUD/SHARED READING

Read aloud the selection to students. Stop periodically for brief discussion of the text. Use the following suggested stopping points and prompts:

- After reading the first paragraph, say: "The author speaks directly to the reader at the beginning. Turn and talk with a partner about whether the author got your attention and why."
- After reading about a rat's whiskers, say: "The author says that a rat uses its whiskers like people use fingers. How does this comparison help you better understand how a rat uses its whiskers?"
- At the end of the selection, say: "How have your feelings about rats changed after reading this selection?"

MINILESSON Fact and Opinion

TEACH Display the minilesson principle on chart paper, and read it aloud to students. Explain that authors often use facts to support their opinions. They present facts that explain how they formed an opinion about something.

1. Discuss the principle with students by using examples from *Frisky Whiskers*. Focus on the author's opinion about rat whiskers. Suggested language: "At the beginning, the author said that a rat's whiskers are *truly amazing*. You know this is an opinion because it cannot be proved. Then the author goes on to support this opinion with facts."

> **MINILESSON PRINCIPLE**
> Readers notice how authors support opinions with facts.

2. Have students name some facts that the author gives to support the opinion that rat whiskers are amazing. (*Its whiskers help it figure out what objects fill its world; they keep it from drowning; they help it "see" in dark tunnels.*)

3. Ask students to tell whether they agree with the author's opinion about rat whiskers. Suggested language: "Do you think the author included enough facts to support his opinion? Why or why not?"

SUMMARIZE AND APPLY Restate the minilesson principle. Tell students to apply it to their independent reading. Suggested language: "When you read, think about the author's opinions and the facts the author uses to support those opinions."

GROUP SHARE Ask students to name an opinion from a selection they read. Have them tell facts the author provided to support that opinion.

▶ In the Wild

INTERACTIVE READ-ALOUD/SHARED READING

Read aloud the play to students. Stop periodically for brief discussion of the text. Use the following suggested stopping points and prompts:

- After reading the first page, ask: "What is Eliza's role in this play?" (*She is a park ranger, and she is trying to explain things about nature to a group of friends.*) Follow-up: "What are the friends doing that is making Eliza's job difficult?" (*They are interrupting her with questions when they see interesting things in the park.*)
- After reading the second page, ask: "What is Eliza trying to teach this group of friends?"
- At the end of the play, ask: "Why do you think the author wrote this play? Turn and talk with a partner about your thinking."

MINILESSON Persuasion

TEACH Display the minilesson principle on chart paper, and read it aloud to students. Explain that you are going to think about how authors try to persuade readers to think or act in a certain way.

1. Discuss the principle with students, using *In the Wild*. Tell students that the author of this play wanted to share a message for readers to learn. Explain that she shared the lesson through the words and actions of the characters.

> **MINILESSON PRINCIPLE**
> Readers notice how the author tries to persuade them to think or act in certain ways.

2. Discuss the example of how the ranger taught the children how to best care for the lost bunny. Suggested language: "In this play, the children learned how to help wild animals in the park. What was it that they learned?" (*They learned not to interfere with the natural balance of nature.*)

3. Guide students to understand that the author wanted to persuade readers to follow the lesson that the characters in the play learned. Have students turn and talk with a partner about what the author would want them to do if they encountered a wild animal in nature.

SUMMARIZE AND APPLY Restate the minilesson principle. Tell students to apply it to their independent reading. Suggested language: "When you read, think about whether the author is trying to persuade you to think or act in a certain way."

GROUP SHARE Ask students to share a selection they have read. Have them tell whether the author tried to persuade them to think or act in a certain way. Then have them tell how they knew.

Whole-Group Lessons • **61**

Whole-Group Lessons

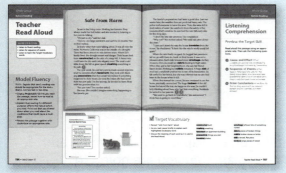

The Earth Dragon Awakes
Student Book, Lesson 12

Safe from Harm
Teacher's Edition, Lesson 12

Texas Twisters
Student Book, Lesson 12

▶ The Earth Dragon Awakes

INTERACTIVE READ-ALOUD/SHARED READING

Read aloud the story to students. Stop periodically for very brief discussion of the text. Use the following suggested stopping points and prompts for quick group response, or give a specific prompt and have partners or threes turn and talk.

- After reading the introduction, ask: "Why does the author put the text in the introduction in different type?" (*to show it's not part of the regular story*)
- After the ceiling drops on Chin and Ah Sing, say: "The author describes the earthquake in so much detail that you feel that you are experiencing it. Turn and talk with a partner about words the author uses to make you see, hear, and feel the earthquake."
- After reading about the city's collapsing buildings, direct attention to the illustration and ask: "How does the illustration give you a better sense of what was happening during the earthquake?"
- At the end of the story, say: "The author doesn't tell you if Chin is able to save his father. Turn and talk with a partner about how the ending makes you feel."

MINILESSON Sequence of Events

TEACH Display the minilesson principle on chart paper, and read it aloud to students. Tell students that they are going to learn about how dates and clue words can help them understand the sequence of events in a story.

1. Discuss the principle with students, using examples from *The Earth Dragon Awakes*. Focus on the introduction to show how the author used dates and other time words to help readers understand the sequence of events. Suggested language: "At the beginning of the story, the author told you what day and time it was to help you understand how much time had passed as you kept reading."
2. Page through the selection with students, pointing out the times and dates shown every few pages.
3. Work with students to find other examples of words the author used to show the sequence of events. Have them look for clue words such as *then* and *until*.
4. Draw on chart paper a Flow Chart like the one shown below. Guide students to identify the most important story events, and have them tell you in which order to write the events in the chart. Ask students to label the events with dates and clue words to show the order of events.

> **MINILESSON PRINCIPLE**
>
> Readers look for dates and clue words to understand the sequence of events.

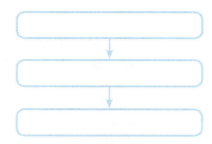

SUMMARIZE AND APPLY Restate the minilesson principle. Then tell students to apply it to their independent reading. Suggested language: "When you read a story, think about how the author uses dates, time, and clue words to help you understand the sequence of events."

GROUP SHARE Ask students to retell a short scene from a story they read, using clue words to explain the order of events.

62 • Lesson 12

Lesson 12

▶ Safe from Harm

INTERACTIVE READ-ALOUD/SHARED READING

Read aloud the story to students. Stop periodically for brief discussion of the text. Use the following suggested stopping points and prompts:

- After reading about how a mudslide could crush Jia's house, say: "Turn and talk with a partner about how the author lets you know that Jia is worried."
- After reading about the wreckage from the mudslide, ask: "How does the author make you feel as he describes what Jia and her parents see when they return to her house?"
- At the end of the story, ask: "Why do you think that Jia is a good friend?"

MINILESSON Sequence of Events

TEACH Display the minilesson principle on chart paper, and read it aloud to students. Tell students that they are going to think about the sequence of events to understand how much time has passed in a story.

1. Discuss the principle with students, using examples from *Safe from Harm*. Remind students that authors have different ways of helping readers understand how much time has passed in a story. Focus on the words *The next week* as you discuss how much time has passed since Jia and her parents talked about the possibility of a mudslide. Suggested language: "The author used the words *The next week* to let readers know that time has passed since the conversation between Jia and her parents."

> **MINILESSON PRINCIPLE**
>
> Readers think about the sequence of events to understand how much time has passed.

2. Work with students to identify other words the author used to help readers know that time has passed, including *just two weeks later* and *for five long days*.

3. Display a Flow Chart on chart paper. Have students explain the order of events in the story as you write them on the chart. Discuss events that happened one right after another, as well as gaps in the story that are explained using clue words and phrases.

SUMMARIZE AND APPLY Restate the minilesson principle. Tell students to apply it to their independent reading. Suggested language: "When you read a story, think about the sequence of events and how the author lets you know that time has passed."

GROUP SHARE Have students tell about the sequence of events in a story they read. Ask them to tell how the author let them know that time had passed in the story.

▶ Texas Twisters

INTERACTIVE READ-ALOUD/SHARED READING

Read aloud the selection to students. Stop periodically for brief discussion of the text. Use the following suggested stopping points and prompts:

- After reading the first page, ask: "What is the author saying about tornadoes and Texas?"
- After reading the section Supercells and Funnel Clouds, ask: "How do meteorologists know a tornado might form?"
- At the end of the selection, ask: "Would you be more concerned to hear about a tornado watch or a tornado warning? Turn and talk with a partner about your thinking."

MINILESSON Genre: Informational Text

TEACH Display the minilesson principle on chart paper, and read it aloud to students. Remind students that authors of informational books use special features like diagrams to give information to readers.

1. Discuss the principle with students, using the section Supercells and Funnel Clouds in *Texas Twisters*. Suggested language: "In this section, the author told you how tornadoes form. The information in the first paragraph was illustrated in the diagram at the bottom of the page."

> **MINILESSON PRINCIPLE**
>
> Readers understand how diagrams can help them understand information.

2. Help students understand that the title of a diagram tells them what kind of information it explains and that labels identify specific parts. Read aloud the labels and have students point to what they refer to.

3. Ask students to use the diagram and the caption to explain in their own words how a tornado forms.

SUMMARIZE AND APPLY Restate the minilesson principle. Tell students to apply it to their independent reading. Suggested language: "When you read, think about the diagrams that authors use to give information. Think about how they help you understand information in the text."

GROUP SHARE Ask students to explain a diagram from a book they read. Tell them to explain how the diagram helped them to understand the information in the book.

Whole-Group Lessons • 63

Whole-Group Lessons

Antarctic Journal: Four Months at the Bottom of the World
Student Book, Lesson 13

On My Way to Meet the Khan: Excerpts from Marco Polo's Adventures
Teacher's Edition, Lesson 13

The Coolest Marathon!
Student Book, Lesson 13

▶ **Antarctic Journal**

INTERACTIVE READ-ALOUD/SHARED READING

Read aloud the selection to students. Stop periodically for very brief discussion of the text. Use the following suggested stopping points and prompts for quick group response, or give a specific prompt and have partners or threes turn and talk.

- After reading the introduction, say: "This selection is a journal. What is a journal?" *(a notebook where you write down what happens each day)*
- After reading the entry from November 27th, ask: "How is a journal organized?" *(by day)* Follow-up: "How does this organization help you understand the information the author tells you?"
- After reading the entry on December 3rd, say: "The author includes a photograph of a penguin. Turn and talk with a partner about how the photograph helps you understand more about the author's experiences."
- At the end of the selection, have students turn and talk with a partner about the most interesting thing they learned about Antarctica.

MINILESSON Cause and Effect

TEACH Display the minilesson principle on chart paper, and read it aloud to students. Tell students that they are going to talk about how authors explain what causes something to happen.

1. Discuss the principle with students, using examples from *Antarctic Journal*. Focus on an event in the selection, such as when penguins argue. Suggested language: "The author told you that penguins will argue and shriek when one penguin steals a stone from the nest of another. The author explained that if one thing happens, then something else happens. *If* is a cause-and-effect clue word."

2. Ask students to point out cause-and-effect relationships in the section dated December 24th. Have one student name a cause and then ask another student to explain the effect.

3. Work with students to identify more examples of cause-and-effect relationships in the selection. Record students' ideas in a T-Map like the one shown here.

> **MINILESSON PRINCIPLE**
>
> Readers notice when the author is explaining what causes something else to happen.

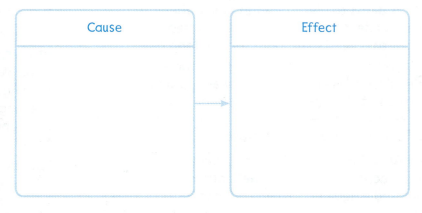

SUMMARIZE AND APPLY Restate the minilesson principle. Then tell students to apply it to their independent reading. Suggested language: "When you read, think about how the author explains what causes something else to happen."

GROUP SHARE Ask students to name an event in a book they read. Have them explain what caused that event to happen.

64 • Lesson 13

Lesson 13

▶ On My Way to Meet the Khan

INTERACTIVE READ-ALOUD/SHARED READING

Read aloud the selection to students. Stop periodically for brief discussion of the text. Use the following suggested stopping points and prompts:

- After reading the introduction, say: "Marco Polo lived a long time ago. How do you think he traveled to China?"
- After reading all the stories, say: "Turn and talk with a partner about which place in China you would like to have seen and explain why."
- At the end of the selection, ask: "How do you think people felt when they heard Marco Polo's tales about China?"

MINILESSON Cause and Effect

TEACH Display the minilesson principle on chart paper, and read it aloud to students. Remind students that certain events cause other events to happen. Tell them that they are going to think about when the author explains what happens as a result of a previous event.

1. Focus on the story in *On My Way to Meet the Khan* that Marco Polo told about the city of Ormus. Suggested language: "The author explained what happened in the city of Ormus in the summer. The wind blew so hot that the people left the city to build homes over the river." Have students identify the cause and the effect in this description, and write them in a T-Map for students to see the relationship.

> **MINILESSON PRINCIPLE**
>
> Readers notice when the author is explaining what happened as a result of a previous event.

2. State another cause-and-effect relationship in the selection. Suggested language: "People stood up to their chins in the river's water because the wind could suffocate them." Ask students to identify the cause and the effect in the statement.

3. Work with students to identify other events that occurred as a result of a previous event. Record students' responses in a T-Map.

SUMMARIZE AND APPLY Restate the minilesson principle. Tell students to apply it to their independent reading. Suggested language: "When you read, think about when the author is explaining what happened as a result of a previous event."

GROUP SHARE Have students name an event that happens in a book they read. Then have them tell whether this event was caused by a previous event.

▶ The Coolest Marathon!

INTERACTIVE READ-ALOUD/SHARED READING

Read aloud the selection to students. Stop periodically for brief discussion of the text. Use the following suggested stopping points and prompts:

- After reading the introduction, ask: "In this introduction, how does the author create excitement about what you are going to read?"
- After reading the section Dashing Through the Snow, ask: "What problems does the author tell about the marathon?"
- At the end of the selection, say: "The selection ends with a blog by a person who actually raced in the marathon. What does this add to the selection? Turn and talk with a partner about your thinking."

MINILESSON Genre: Informational Text

TEACH Display the minilesson principle on chart paper, and read it aloud to students. Explain to students that when readers come across a word they don't know, they use the words and sentences around the unknown word as clues to figure out what it means.

1. Discuss the principle with students, drawing vocabulary from *The Coolest Marathon!* Focus on the term *wind chills* on the first page. Guide students to understand how they can figure out the meaning. Suggested language: "If you didn't know what the term *wind chills* meant, you could read the rest of the sentence for clues. The sentence tells you that wind chills are as low as 40 degrees below zero. That clue helps you to know that wind chills are something like *temperature*."

> **MINILESSON PRINCIPLE**
>
> Readers notice new vocabulary and use clues to figure out the meanings of words.

2. Work with students to use clues to figure out the meaning of the following words from the selection: *crevasses, variable, headwind*.

SUMMARIZE AND APPLY Restate the minilesson principle. Tell students to apply it to their independent reading. Suggested language: "When you read, use clues to figure out the meaning of vocabulary words you don't know."

GROUP SHARE Have students name a word they did not know from a book they read. Tell them to explain how they figured out its meaning.

Whole-Group Lessons • **65**

Whole-Group Lessons

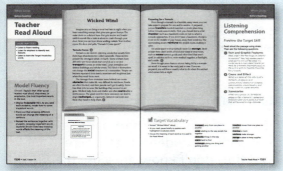

The Life and Times of the Ant
Student Book, Lesson 14

Wicked Wind
Teacher's Edition, Lesson 14

The Dove and the Ant
Student Book, Lesson 14

▶ **The Life and Times of the Ant**

INTERACTIVE READ-ALOUD/SHARED READING

Read aloud the selection to students. Stop periodically for very brief discussion of the text. Use the following suggested stopping points and prompts for quick group response, or give a specific prompt and have partners or threes turn and talk.

- After reading the section Masters of the Earth, ask: "How does the author describe ants?" Follow-up: "Why does the author call them *masters of the earth?*"
- After reading the section A Life of Work, ask: "How is the information in this section organized?" *(It is organized by types of ants and their jobs.)* Follow-up: "How does this organization help you understand the information?"
- After reading the section A Dangerous World, say: "The author tells about some of the dangers that ants face in a big world. Turn and talk with a partner about what you think ants see when they look out at the world."
- At the end of the selection, ask students to turn and tell a partner about the most interesting thing they learned about ants.

MINILESSON Text and Graphic Features

TEACH Display the minilesson principle on chart paper, and read it aloud to students. Tell students that they are going to learn how using text and graphic features can help them learn more about a topic as they read.

1. Discuss the principle with students, using examples of text and graphic features from *The Life and Times of the Ant*. Suggested language: "In the selection, the author used different kinds of writing and graphic features to help you learn more information about ants. What were some of these features?" *(headings, diagrams, illustrations, charts, timeline)*

2. Focus on the diagram of the anteater. Suggested language: "The author used a diagram of an anteater to give you information about what anteaters do. What specific information did the diagram show?" *(It showed how each part of the anteater's body helps it hunt for ants.)*

3. Point out how the diagram's callouts highlight the different parts of the anteater's body. Ask partners to select one callout and discuss how it helps them understand anteaters.

4. Work with students to identify more examples of text and graphic features from the selection. Record students' ideas in a T-Map like the one shown here.

MINILESSON PRINCIPLE

Readers use text and graphic features to help them learn more about the topic.

Text or Graphic Feature	Information It Gives Readers

SUMMARIZE AND APPLY Restate the minilesson principle. Explain to students that they should notice text and graphic features as they read. Suggested language: "When you read, think about the text and graphic features the author uses to give information. Think about how it helps you understand more about the topic."

GROUP SHARE Ask students to share what they noticed about one text or graphic feature in their reading. Tell them to explain what the feature is and the information it gives.

66 • Lesson 14

Lesson 14

▶ Wicked Wind

INTERACTIVE READ-ALOUD/SHARED READING

Read aloud the selection to students. Stop periodically for brief discussion of the text. Use the following suggested stopping points and prompts:

- After reading the introduction, ask: "How does the author get your attention with this first paragraph?" *(by talking directly to the reader and telling exactly what you might see and hear as a tornado approaches)*
- After reading the section Tornado Forces, say: "The author tells how tornadoes affect survivors. Turn and talk with a partner about how you might help people who have survived a tornado."
- At the end of the selection, ask: "What do you think is the best advice the author gives to help people prepare for tornadoes?"

MINILESSON Genre: Informational Text

TEACH Display the minilesson principle on chart paper, and read it aloud to students. Tell students that they are going to learn about how the author's description helps them understand what something is like.

1. Explain to students that authors use precise words to help readers "see" and "hear" what is being described. Using *Wicked Wind*, discuss the author's description of the sound of a tornado. Suggested language: "In the first paragraph, the author described how a tornado sounds. What words did the author use to help you imagine how tornadoes sound?" *(a distant hum that gets louder and louder; a train that is about to crash through your door)*

> **MINILESSON PRINCIPLE**
>
> Readers think about the author's description of something to understand how it looks and sounds.

2. Have students identify other words in the selection that describe what a tornado is like. *(violent, spinning, huge, large, destroy, damage, scary)* Display students' ideas in a Web labeled *Tornado*.

SUMMARIZE AND APPLY Restate the minilesson principle. Tell students that when they read, they should think about the descriptions authors give. Suggested language: "When you read, think about how the author describes how things look and sound to help you understand what they are like."

GROUP SHARE Ask students to share a description they found in their reading that explains how something looks or sounds.

▶ The Dove and the Ant

INTERACTIVE READ-ALOUD/SHARED READING

Read aloud the story to students. Stop periodically for brief discussion of the text. Use the following suggested stopping points and prompts:

- After the Dove tells the Ant about the river, ask: "How does the author show what the Dove and the Ant are like?" Follow-up: "Which character would you rather have as a friend?"
- After the Ant gets back on shore, say: "The ant seems really grateful for the Dove's help. What does she mean when she says *Life is hard and such kindness is scarce?*"
- At the end of the story, have students turn and talk with a partner about how the Ant and the Dove are alike.

MINILESSON Genre: Fable

TEACH Display the minilesson principle on chart paper, and read it aloud to students. Then reread with students the introduction of *The Dove and the Ant*, emphasizing that it is fable.

1. Introduce students to the idea that fables are written to teach readers a lesson about life. Explain to students that knowing what to expect when they read a fable will help them understand what they read. Suggested language: "In the story, the Ant learned a lesson when the Dove saved her life. Sometimes readers apply a story's lesson to their own lives in different ways. What lesson did you take away from reading the fable?" *(We can make friends by doing kind things for others.)*

> **MINILESSON PRINCIPLE**
>
> Readers think about the lesson or moral in a fable.

2. Point out to students that the author used story details such as the characters' traits and what they did to explain the lesson. Guide students to identify story details that supported the author's message about being kind.

SUMMARIZE AND APPLY Restate the minilesson principle. Then ask students to apply it to their independent reading. Suggested language: "When you read fables, think about the lesson or moral of the story."

GROUP SHARE Ask students to share a lesson they learned from a story they read. Tell them to explain how details in the story were used to teach the lesson.

Whole-Group Lessons • **67**

Whole-Group Lessons

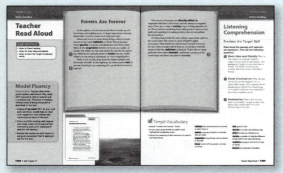

Ecology for Kids
Student Book, Lesson 15

Forests Are Forever
Teacher's Edition, Lesson 15

Wonderful Weather
Student Book, Lesson 15

▶ **Ecology for Kids**

INTERACTIVE READ-ALOUD/SHARED READING

Read aloud the selection to students. Stop periodically for very brief discussion of the text. Use the following suggested stopping points and prompts for quick group response, or give a specific prompt and have partners or threes turn and talk.

- After reading the section Ecology, ask: "What do you predict you will learn from reading this selection?" Have students turn and talk with a partner about their predictions.
- After reading the section Destruction of the Forests, ask: "How does the author organize the information in the selection?" Follow-up: "How do the headings help you find information?"
- After reading the section An Ocean of Resources, ask: "What is similar about this section and the section about forests that we read before it?" *(They both tell about important resources and how we should use them.)*
- At the end of the selection, say: "The author ends the selection with ideas about how you can protect Earth. Turn and talk with a partner about why you think he includes this information."

MINILESSON Main Ideas and Details

TEACH Display the minilesson principle on chart paper, and read it aloud to students. Tell students that they are going to learn about how to use details in a selection to figure out what the main idea is. Explain that the main idea is what a text is mostly about.

1. Discuss the principle with students, using examples from *Ecology for Kids*. Suggested language: "In the section Ecosystem, the author gave you a lot of details about ecosystems and the things that live in them. These details all told about the main idea. The main idea of this section is that an ecosystem is a natural area where living and nonliving things live and interact with each other. This is what the section is mostly about."

> **MINILESSON PRINCIPLE**
> Readers use details in a text to figure out the main idea, or what a text is mostly about.

2. Work with students to name the main idea of the other sections of the selection. Have them identify details in the text that helped them identify the main idea.
3. Record students' responses in an Idea-Support Map like the one shown here.

SUMMARIZE AND APPLY Restate the minilesson principle. Then tell students to apply it to their independent reading. Suggested language: "When you read, think about the details the author gives to help you figure out the main ideas."

GROUP SHARE Ask students to name a main idea from a book they read. Then have them name details that helped them figure out what the main idea was.

68 • Lesson 15

Lesson 15

▶ Forests Are Forever

INTERACTIVE READ-ALOUD/SHARED READING

Read aloud the selection to students. Stop periodically for brief discussion of the text. Use the following suggested stopping points and prompts:

- After reading the first paragraph, ask: "How does the author's introduction make you curious about forests?"
- After reading about how people can affect a forest in good ways, ask: "What are some other ways that people can affect a forest in a good way? Turn and talk with a partner about your thinking."
- At the end of the selection, ask: "What is the most important thing you learned from the selection?"

MINILESSON Main Ideas and Details

TEACH Display the minilesson principle on chart paper, and read it aloud to students. Tell students that authors often state the main idea of a paragraph in the first or last sentence. Then explain that in some cases, authors do not state the main idea at all, but they expect readers to figure it out using details provided.

1. Focus on the second paragraph of *Forests Are Forever*, and reread it aloud to students. Guide them to understand that the main idea of this paragraph is stated in the first sentence: *Forests are home to many living things.* Have students name details in the paragraph that tell about this main idea.

> **MINILESSON PRINCIPLE**
>
> Readers notice that the author's main idea may be stated or unstated.

2. Next, focus on the last paragraph, and reread it aloud to students. Tell students that the main idea of this paragraph is not stated. Suggested language: "The author doesn't directly state the main idea of this paragraph. You have to think about the details in the paragraph and figure out the main idea. The main idea of this paragraph is: *The ozone layer needs to be saved in order to protect the planet.*" Have students name details the author gives that tell about this main idea. Record their responses in an Idea-Support Map.

SUMMARIZE AND APPLY Restate the minilesson principle. Tell students to apply it to their independent reading. Suggested language: "When you read, think about what the main idea is. Think about whether the author states the main idea or expects you to figure it out."

GROUP SHARE Have students name a main idea from a book they read. Have them tell whether the main idea was stated or unstated.

▶ Wonderful Weather

INTERACTIVE READ-ALOUD/SHARED READING

Read aloud the poems to students. Stop periodically for brief discussion. Use the following suggested stopping points and prompts:

- After reading the poem "Lightning Bolt," ask: "How does the way the poet arranges the words in this poem make it fun to read?"
- After reading the poem "Weather," ask: "What is special about the words that the poet uses to tell about weather sounds?" *(The words sound like the different kinds of weather.)*
- After the last poem, say: "Each poem tells about weather in a different way. Which poem do you think is most memorable? Turn and talk about your thinking with a partner."

MINILESSON Genre: Poetry

TEACH Display the minilesson principle on chart paper, and read it aloud to students. Explain to students that they are going to learn how rhyming words give poems rhythm and form.

1. Read aloud "Lightning Bolt" to students, emphasizing the rhythm and rhyme. Guide them to understand how the rhyming words *key* and *electricity* help to give the poem rhythm. Suggested language: "Poems often have rhyming words in them. When you read a poem, these rhyming words help to give the poems a musical feeling, or rhythm."

> **MINILESSON PRINCIPLE**
>
> Readers notice how rhyming words give a poem rhythm and form.

2. Have students identify the rhyming words in "Weather." Have them take turns reading the poem and emphasizing the rhyming words. Discuss how the rhyming words help to give the poem its rhythm.

3. Last, discuss the poem "Umbrella." Explain that in this poem, the rhyming words fall at the end of lines. Suggested language: "Rhyming words often fall at the end of a line in a poem. They give the poem its form."

SUMMARIZE AND APPLY Restate the minilesson principle. Tell students to apply it to their independent reading. Suggested language: "When you read a poem, think about how the rhyming words give it rhythm and form."

GROUP SHARE Ask students to share a poem they have read. Tell them to name the rhyming words in it. Then have them read aloud a few lines from the poem to show its rhythm and form.

Whole-Group Lessons • **69**

Whole-Group Lessons

Riding Freedom
Student Book, Lesson 16

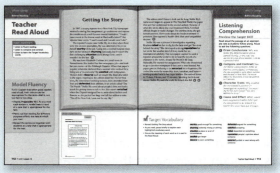

Getting the Story
Teacher's Edition, Lesson 16

Spindletop
Student Book, Lesson 16

▶ **Riding Freedom**

INTERACTIVE READ-ALOUD/SHARED READING

Read aloud the story to students. Stop periodically for very brief discussion of the text. Use the following suggested stopping points and prompts for quick group response, or give a specific prompt and have partners or threes turn and talk.

- After Charlotte sets a goal to have ten good round-trip runs, ask: "What can you tell so far about the main character of this story?" *(She is determined; she sets a goal and works hard to achieve it.)*
- After James agrees to let Charlotte drive, ask: "What do you think will happen when James watches Charlotte drive the stagecoach?"
- After Charlotte checks the bridge, ask: "What is Charlotte's plan for crossing the bridge?"
- At the end of the story, say: "The passengers in the stage thought Charlotte was a boy. What do you think they would have done if they knew the truth? Turn and talk about your thinking with a partner."

MINILESSON Genre: Historical Fiction

TEACH Display the minilesson principle on chart paper, and read it aloud to students. Explain that in historical fiction, the setting is important to what happens in the story. The events happen in a time and a real place in the past. Tell students they will learn to notice details about the setting that help them recognize that a story is historical fiction.

1. Discuss the principle, using examples from *Riding Freedom*. Suggested language: "In the introduction, you found out that the story took place in the 1800s, when girls were not allowed to have paid jobs. This tells you that the story happened in the past."

2. Have a volunteer reread the introduction aloud, and ask students to listen for other details about the setting. Ask them to share what they discovered as you write the details in a Web like the one shown below.

> **MINILESSON PRINCIPLE**
>
> Readers notice that the setting in historical fiction is a time and a real place in the past.

3. Focus students' attention on other details in the story that describe the setting. Ask: "What other details in the story helped you understand that the story happened in the past?" *(people used horses for transportation, a stagecoach delivered mail and brought passengers from place to place)* Continue adding to the Web as students explain their findings.

SUMMARIZE AND APPLY Restate the minilesson principle. Then tell students to apply it to their independent reading. Suggested language: "When you read, notice details about the setting that explain where and when the story takes place. Think about how the setting helps you understand what kind of story you are reading."

GROUP SHARE Ask students to share details about setting from their reading that helped them understand what kind of story they read.

70 • Lesson 16

Lesson 16

▶ Getting the Story

INTERACTIVE READ-ALOUD/SHARED READING

Read aloud the biography to students. Stop periodically for brief discussion of the text. Use the following suggested stopping points and prompts:

- After reading the first page, ask: "What was it like when Nellie Bly lived?" *(Many women didn't work, and many people didn't accept the idea of it.)*
- After reading that Nellie Bly was an investigative reporter, say: "Why do you think the kinds of stories that Nellie Bly wrote were called investigative reporting? Turn and talk about your ideas with a partner."
- At the end of the selection, ask: "Throughout her life, how did Nellie Bly react when people told her she couldn't do something?"

MINILESSON Genre: Biography

TEACH Display the minilesson principle on chart paper, and read it aloud to students. Tell students that the subject of a biography—the real person that the writing is about—often accomplished something in life that other people may find interesting or even inspiring. Explain that thinking about what a subject tried to do and why it was important can help them understand more about the subject's life.

1. Discuss the principle, using examples from *Getting the Story*. Suggested language: "The author wrote that Nellie Bly quit her job because she wasn't satisfied with writing about fashion and flowers. She wanted to write about more important things. Why do you think this is important? Turn and talk about your thinking with a partner."

> **MINILESSON PRINCIPLE**
>
> Readers think about what a subject tried to do and why it was important.

2. Discuss Nellie Bly's accomplishments with students, and have them explain why the accomplishments were important. Ask: "Why were the things Nellie did important to others?" *(She proved that women could be good journalists. She wrote the kind of stories that caused change.)*

SUMMARIZE AND APPLY Restate the minilesson principle. Tell students to apply it to their independent reading. Suggested language: "When you read, think about what the subject tried to do and why it was important."

GROUP SHARE Ask students to share an example of a biography they read. Have them tell what the person tried to do and why it was important.

▶ Spindletop

INTERACTIVE READ-ALOUD/SHARED READING

Read aloud the selection to students. Stop periodically for brief discussion of the text. Use the following suggested stopping points and prompts:

- After reading the first page, ask: "Why do you believe Pattillo Higgins thought that Spindletop was an important area to explore?"
- After Lucas finds oil, ask: "What was so important about Lucas's discovery?" *(The oil field produced more barrels of oil than any other oil field in Texas.)*
- After reading the last page, ask: "What information does the e-mail add to the selection? Why do you think the author includes it?"

MINILESSON Compare and Contrast

TEACH Display the minilesson principle on chart paper, and read it aloud to students. Tell students that they are going to learn to think about similarities and differences in two different selections. Explain that thinking about how selections are alike and different will help them recognize when one book they read reminds them of another book they have read.

1. Remind students that in *Riding Freedom* and *Spindletop*, they read about several people who faced challenges. Have students recall that in both selections the characters had to convince others to believe in them. Point out that this is a similarity between the selections.

> **MINILESSON PRINCIPLE**
>
> Readers look for similarities and differences between two texts they read.

2. Ask students to explain how the challenges that the people faced in *Riding Freedom* and *Spindletop* were different. Ask: "What was different about the people in these selections?" Record students' responses in a Venn Diagram.

3. Have students volunteer other similarities and differences between the two selections as you add their ideas to the Venn Diagram. Tell students to think about genre, characters' traits, and text features.

SUMMARIZE AND APPLY Restate the minilesson principle, and tell students to apply it to their independent reading. Suggested language: "When you read, look for similarities and differences between what you are reading and something you've read before."

GROUP SHARE Ask students to share how two books they read are alike and different.

Whole-Group Lessons • 71

Whole-Group Lessons

The Right Dog for the Job: Ira's Path from Service Dog to Guide Dog
Student Book, Lesson 17

Let Me Be Brave
Teacher's Edition, Lesson 17

The Sticky Coyote
Student Book, Lesson 17

▶ The Right Dog for the Job

INTERACTIVE READ-ALOUD/SHARED READING

Read aloud the selection to students. Stop periodically for very brief discussion of the text. Use the following suggested stopping points and prompts for quick group response, or give a specific prompt and have partners or threes turn and talk.

- After reading the first two pages, ask: "Why do you think the training of service dogs is so important?" Follow-up: "Why is something like picking up keys important for service dogs to learn?"
- After reading the section in which Ira completes his training to become a service dog, ask: "What qualities does a service dog need to have?" Follow-up: "Turn and talk with a partner about why you think these qualities are important."
- After reading about the graduation, ask: "How do you think Sandy feels at the graduation?" Follow-up: "How do you think Don feels?"
- After reading the selection, remind students that authors have a reason, or purpose, for writing. Ask: "Why do you think the author wrote this selection? Turn and talk about your thinking with a partner."

MINILESSON Sequence of Events

TEACH Display the minilesson principle on chart paper, and read it aloud to students. Tell students that noticing how the author organizes information and why can help them recognize what is most important about a selection.

1. Discuss the principle with students, using examples from *The Right Dog for the Job*. Focus on the first paragraph. Suggested language: "The author began by telling you about the place where Ira was born and what he was like. This is a clue that information is organized in the order things happened."

> **MINILESSON PRINCIPLE**
> Readers notice how the author organizes information and why.

2. Remind students that time-order words and phrases are clues that information is organized by the sequence of events. Ask students to point out time-order words and phrases on the first two pages of the selection.
3. On chart paper, draw a Flow Chart, and explain to students that they will identify important events in the selection as you write them in the chart. Tell students to focus on the key parts of Irah's training.
4. Ask students to turn and talk with a partner about why the organization of this selection makes sense for the topic. Tell them to think about how the organization helps them understand the dogs' training.

SUMMARIZE AND APPLY Restate the minilesson principle. Then tell students to apply it to their independent reading. Suggested language: "When you read, notice how the author organizes the text. Think about how it helps you understand the information."

GROUP SHARE Ask students to explain how the author organized the information in a book they read. Have them tell why they think the author organized it that way.

Lesson 17

▶ Let Me Be Brave

INTERACTIVE READ-ALOUD/SHARED READING

Read aloud the biography to students. Stop periodically for brief discussion of the text. Use the following suggested stopping points and prompts:

- After reading that Liinah's father died, ask: "What difficult decision did Liinah have to make?" Follow-up: "Why do you think she made the decision that she did?"
- After reading about the Irish social workers who are at Liinah's race, ask: "Do you think the tragedy in Liinah's life will affect her race? Why or why not?"
- At the end of the selection, ask: "Why do you think the author wrote about Liinah? Turn and talk about your thinking with a partner."

MINILESSON Sequence of Events

TEACH Display the minilesson principle on chart paper, and read it aloud to students. Tell students they will learn how clue words can help them understand the sequence of events.

1. Discuss the principle with students, using examples from *Let Me Be Brave*. Read aloud the second paragraph again, and ask students to raise their hand when they hear a clue word that indicates sequence.

> **MINILESSON PRINCIPLE**
>
> Readers look for clue words to understand the sequence of events.

2. Tell students that dates and other clues about time can also help to explain the sequence of events. Point out the example *just two months before*.

3. Have students turn and talk with a partner to retell the events in Liinah Bukenya's life that led up to the 2003 Special Olympics. Tell them to use clue words to explain the sequence of events.

SUMMARIZE AND APPLY Restate the minilesson principle. Tell students to apply it to their independent reading. Suggested language: "When you read, look for clue words to understand the sequence of events."

GROUP SHARE Ask students to share a book they read. Have them explain how the author used clue words to help them understand the sequence of events.

▶ The Sticky Coyote

INTERACTIVE READ-ALOUD/SHARED READING

Read aloud the play to students. Stop periodically for brief discussion of the text. Use the following suggested stopping points and prompts:

- After the first page, ask: "Based on what you know about Coyote so far, what do you think he will do to the Shoemaker?"
- After reading the second page, ask: "What is the narrator's role in this play?" *(The narrator tells about the action and gives information that is not included in the dialogue.)*
- At the end of the play, ask: "Do you think Coyote will ever truly learn his lesson? Turn and talk about your thinking with a partner."

MINILESSON Genre: Trickster Tale

TEACH Display the minilesson principle on chart paper, and read it aloud to students. Explain to students that a trickster tale is a kind of folktale. In a trickster tale, a mischievous character called the trickster tries to fool the other characters for his own gain.

1. Discuss the principle with students by using examples from *The Sticky Coyote*. Focus on the narrator's description of Coyote. Suggested language: "The narrator said that Coyote liked to disobey rules and play tricks on people. This tells you that Coyote is a trickster."

> **MINILESSON PRINCIPLE**
>
> Readers notice that a trickster is a character who tries to fool other characters.

2. Have students explain the motive for Coyote's trick in the story. Suggested language: "Coyote wanted to avoid being captured by the villagers, so he came up with a plan to trick them. What did he do?"

3. Explain to students that tricksters sometimes end up getting tricked themselves. Suggested language: "Sometimes a trickster's actions will backfire, and the trickster is the one who is fooled. What did Coyote do to try to fool another character?" Follow-up: "How was Coyote fooled instead?"

SUMMARIZE AND APPLY Restate the minilesson principle. Tell students to apply it to their independent reading. Suggested language: "When you read, notice if any of the characters are tricksters. Think about how the trickster tries to fool other characters."

GROUP SHARE Ask students to tell about a trickster from a story they read.

Whole-Group Lessons • 73

Whole-Group Lessons

Moon Runner
Student Book, Lesson 18

Darnell Tries Harder
Teacher's Edition, Lesson 18

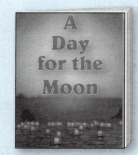

A Day for the Moon
Student Book, Lesson 18

▶ Moon Runner

INTERACTIVE READ-ALOUD/SHARED READING

Read aloud the story to students. Stop periodically for very brief discussion of the text. Use the following suggested stopping points and prompts for quick group response, or give a specific prompt and have partners or threes turn and talk.

- After reading the introduction, say: "What do you think will happen in this story?" Follow-up: "What do you think will happen to Ruth and Mina's friendship?"
- After Ruth suggests the two girls race each other, ask: "Why is Mina afraid to beat Ruth in a race?" *(She is afraid it will ruin their friendship.)* Follow-up: "In their race, do you think Mina will run her hardest or let Ruth win?"
- At the end of the selection, ask: "What does Mina learn from Ruth? What does Ruth learn from Mina? Turn and talk about your thinking with a partner."

MINILESSON Understanding Characters

TEACH Display the minilesson principle on chart paper, and read it aloud to students. Tell students that characters often change as a result of things that happen or challenges they face in the story. Explain that noticing how a character changes and why will help them to understand a story better.

1. Discuss the principle, using examples from *Moon Runner*. Suggested language: "At the beginning of the story, Mina said she was a *girlie girl,* not a real athlete. What did this tell you about what Mina is like?"

2. Next, discuss with students what Mina was like at the end of the story. Suggested language: "Think about what Mina was like at the end of the story. What did she say and do? How did the race with Ruth make her feel?"

3. Talk with students about how Mina changed and the things that happened in the story that caused her to change. Record their ideas in a Column Chart like the one shown here. Repeat the steps to show how Ruth changed.

> **MINILESSON PRINCIPLE**
>
> Readers notice how characters in a story change and why.

Beginning	Middle	End

SUMMARIZE AND APPLY Restate the minilesson principle. Then tell students to apply it to their independent reading. Suggested language: "When you read, notice how the characters in the story change and why."

GROUP SHARE Ask students to tell about a character in a story they read. Have them tell how that character changed and why.

Lesson 18

▶ Darnell Tries Harder

INTERACTIVE READ-ALOUD/SHARED READING

Read aloud the story to students. Stop periodically for brief discussion of the text. Use the following suggested stopping points and prompts:

- After reading the first page, ask: "How does Darnell feel when he sees his sister climb the hill?" (*He is jealous of her.*) Follow-up: "Why do you think climbing the hill is important to Darnell?"
- After Lannie passes Darnell on his bike, ask: "What does Darnell do when Lannie passes him?" (*He becomes more determined to get up the hill.*) Follow-up: "What does that tell you about the kind of person Darnell is?"
- At the end of the selection, ask: "How do you think Darnell feels now?" Follow-up: "How is the hill almost like a character in this story? Turn and talk with a partner about your ideas."

MINILESSON Compare and Contrast

TEACH Display the minilesson principle on chart paper, and read it aloud to students. Explain that thinking about how stories they have read are alike and different will help them understand and enjoy what they read. Tell students that they are going to look for how characters in different stories are alike and different.

1. Ask students to summarize the stories *Moon Runner* and *Darnell Tries Harder*. Then tell students that when they read a story, they may notice that a character reminds them of a character they have read about in a different story.

> **MINILESSON PRINCIPLE**
>
> Readers look for similarities and differences between characters in different stories.

2. Focus students' attention on *Darnell Tries Harder*. Suggested language: "Who was the main character in *Darnell Tries Harder*?" Follow-up: "What was Darnell's goal in this story?"
3. Repeat the process for *Moon Runner,* focusing on the character of Mina.
4. Have students explain how Mina and Darnell were alike and different by talking about their goals, challenges, and the final outcome. Record their responses in a Venn Diagram.

SUMMARIZE AND APPLY Restate the minilesson principle. Tell students to apply it to their independent reading. Suggested language: "When you read, think about how the characters are similar to and different from characters in other stories."

GROUP SHARE Ask students to tell about a character in a story they read. Have them tell how that character is similar to or different from a character in another story.

▶ A Day for the Moon

INTERACTIVE READ-ALOUD/SHARED READING

Read aloud the selection to students. Stop periodically for brief discussion of the text. Use the following suggested stopping points and prompts:

- After reading the section The Legend of Chang E, say: "A legend is a story that is told as if it were true. What parts of this legend help you know that it could not really happen? Turn and talk with a partner about your thinking."
- After reading the section Lanterns and Moon Cakes, say: "The author tells us that the festival is filled with customs. What examples does the author use to support this statement?"
- At the end of the selection, ask: "Why do you think the author includes the information at the end of the selection?"

MINILESSON Compare and Contrast

TEACH Display the minilesson principle on chart paper, and read it aloud to students. Tell students that comparing things they are learning about to things they have experienced in their own lives can help them understand a topic better.

1. Discuss the principle with students, using examples from *A Day for the Moon*. Suggested language: "People celebrate different holidays and have different customs. Holidays from different cultures have similarities and differences. How is the Moon Festival similar to a holiday that you celebrate or one you have read about?"

> **MINILESSON PRINCIPLE**
>
> Readers make comparisons between what they read and their own experiences.

2. Next, ask students to think about what makes the Moon Festival different from any other holiday. Elicit from students that it is the only holiday that celebrates the Chinese legend of Chang E. Encourage students to name unique characteristics of other holidays.
3. Select one holiday that students have named, and work with them to explain the how it is similar to and different from the Moon Festival. Display students' responses in a Venn Diagram.

SUMMARIZE AND APPLY Restate the minilesson principle. Tell students to apply it to their independent reading. Suggested language: "When you read, compare what you are reading about to something you have experienced."

GROUP SHARE Ask students to share an example of something they read about that is similar to something they have experienced in their own lives. Have them tell how they are the same.

Whole-Group Lessons • 75

Whole-Group Lessons

Harvesting Hope: The Story of Cesar Chavez
Student Book, Lesson 19

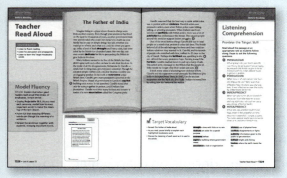

The Father of India
Teacher's Edition, Lesson 19

The Edible Schoolyard
Student Book, Lesson 19

▶ **Harvesting Hope**

INTERACTIVE READ-ALOUD/SHARED READING

Read aloud the biography to students. Stop periodically for very brief discussion of the text. Use the following suggested stopping points and prompts for quick group response, or give a specific prompt and have partners or threes turn and talk.

- After reading the introduction, say: "This selection is a biography. How is a biography different from a story?"
- After reading about the family earning thirty cents a day for their work, ask: "What was Cesar's life like when he began traveling from one farm to another for work?"
- After the first meeting Cesar has with other workers, say: "Why do you think Cesar feels strongly about the idea of nonviolence?"
- At the end of the selection, remind students that Cesar Chavez did not think violence could help solve problems. Then say: "Do you agree or disagree? Turn and talk about your thinking with a partner."

MINILESSON Genre: Biography

TEACH Display the minilesson principle on chart paper, and read it aloud to students. Tell students that people in different parts of the world and in different times face different problems. Remind students that in a biography, the setting is a real place. Then tell students that they are going to think about how the place where the subject of a biography lives can affect the person's life.

1. Discuss the principle with students, using examples from *Harvesting Hope*. Suggested language: "When Cesar was a boy, he lived on a ranch in Arizona. He learned what it was like to work on a farm."

2. Contrast Cesar's life in Arizona to his life as a migrant worker. Suggested language: "Cesar's life changed when he moved to California. Why were the conditions that he worked in such a shock?"

3. Guide students to understand how Cesar's life changed when he moved from Arizona to California. Point out that the place where he lived inspired him to fight for better working conditions. Have students give details about what California was like and how it affected Cesar. Record students' ideas in an Idea-Support Map like the one shown here.

> **MINILESSON PRINCIPLE**
>
> Readers think about the setting of a biography and how it affected the person's life.

SUMMARIZE AND APPLY Restate the minilesson principle. Then tell students to apply it to their independent reading. Suggested language: "When you read a biography, think about the setting and how it affects the person's life."

GROUP SHARE Ask students to tell about a person from a biography they have read. Have them tell how the setting affected that person's life.

76 • Lesson 19

Lesson 19

▶ The Father of India

INTERACTIVE READ-ALOUD/SHARED READING

Read aloud the biography to students. Stop periodically for brief discussion of the text. Use the following suggested stopping points and prompts:

- After reading the first paragraph, ask: "How does the author help you imagine what it used to be like to live in India?"
- After reading the first page, ask: "Why do you think the author tells you that Gandhi wore simple clothes and had a modest lifestyle? Turn and talk about your thinking with a partner."
- At the end of the selection, ask: "Why do you think Gandhi's strategies to create change influenced other people?"

MINILESSON Persuasion

TEACH Display the minilesson principle on chart paper, and read it aloud to students. Tell students that sometimes an author's goal is to persuade readers to think or act a certain way. Explain that in a biography, an author may want readers to agree with an opinion about the subject.

1. Discuss the principle with students, using examples from *The Father of India*. Explain to students that authors of biographies write about their subject because they believe the person did something important and that other people could learn from the person's life. They want readers to agree that the person is important.

   > **MINILESSON PRINCIPLE**
   >
   > Readers think about how well the author shows that the subject is important.

2. Ask students to explain how they know that the author of *The Father of India* believed that Gandhi was an important person.

3. Work with students to develop a list that shows the author's supporting evidence for the opinion. Then ask students whether the author provided enough evidence to persuade them to agree with the author's opinion.

SUMMARIZE AND APPLY Restate the minilesson principle. Tell students to apply it to their independent reading. Suggested language: "When you read, think about the author's opinion about the subject. Think about how well the author shows that the subject is important."

GROUP SHARE Ask students to describe a person they have read about. Have them give examples of how the author shows that the person is important.

▶ The Edible Schoolyard

INTERACTIVE READ-ALOUD/SHARED READING

Read aloud the selection to students. Stop periodically for brief discussion of the text. Use the following suggested stopping points and prompts:

- After reading the introduction, ask: "What do you think happens in the Edible Schoolyard?"
- After reading the section Time to Get Cooking, say: "Students who work in the garden learn about different foods, but they also learn to work together. Turn and talk with a partner about how the garden teaches them many important skills."
- At the end of the selection, ask: "Do you agree with the author that the Edible Garden is *part garden, part kitchen, and part classroom*? Support your thinking with ideas in the text."

MINILESSON Genre: Informational Text

TEACH Display the minilesson principle on chart paper, and read it aloud to students. Remind them that informational texts like *The Edible Schoolyard* give information about a topic. Explain to students that authors often include pictures, graphs, and other visuals that relate to information in the text in order to help readers understand the topic and why it is important.

1. Direct students' attention to the graph on the last page. Tell students that when they see a graph, they should first think about what it shows. Suggested language: "What does the information in the graph help you understand?" *(what foods are healthy and how much people should eat each day)*

   > **MINILESSON PRINCIPLE**
   >
   > Readers notice information shown in graphs and how it relates to the text.

2. Have students summarize what the Edible Schoolyard is and why it is important. Then tell students to think about how the graph relates to the ideas in the main text. Suggested language: "How does the graph relate to the information in the text?" *(It shows that the foods the students are growing in the garden are healthy. The fruits and vegetables they grow are part of the diet recommended by the U.S. government.)*

SUMMARIZE AND APPLY Restate the minilesson principle. Tell students to apply it to their independent reading. Suggested language: "When you read, notice how information in a graph relates to the text. Think about how the graph helps you understand more about the topic."

GROUP SHARE Ask students to share an example of a graph from their reading. Have them tell how it relates to the text.

Whole-Group Lessons • 77

Whole-Group Lessons

Sacagawea
Student Book, Lesson 20

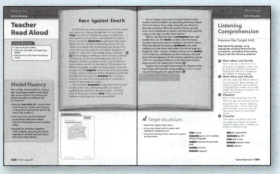

Race Against Death
Teacher's Edition, Lesson 20

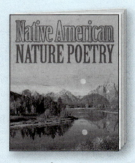

Native American Nature Poetry
Student Book, Lesson 20

▶ Sacagawea

INTERACTIVE READ-ALOUD/SHARED READING

Read aloud the biography to students. Stop periodically for very brief discussion of the text. Use the following suggested stopping points and prompts for quick group response, or give a specific prompt and have partners or threes turn and talk.

- After reading that Charbonneau and Sacagawea will join the Corps, ask: "How have the lives of the two different groups now joined? What experience will they share?"
- After Sacagawea rescues the captains' supplies, ask: "How do you think the captains felt about having Sacagawea on the journey?" Follow-up: "How did they show their appreciation?"
- After the explorers reach the Pacific Ocean, ask: "What do you think it was like for Sacagawea to go on this journey?" Have students use examples from the selection to support their answers.
- At the end of the selection, ask: "How can you tell that the captains respected Sacagawea by the end of the journey? Turn and talk with a partner about your thinking."

MINILESSON Main Ideas and Details

TEACH Display the minilesson principle on chart paper, and read it aloud to students. Tell students that they are going to learn about how to use details in a text to figure out the main idea.

1. Discuss the principle with students, using examples from *Sacagawea*. Suggested language: "The main idea of a story is what the story is mostly about. The author supports the main idea with important details. What are some important details in this story?" As students give their responses, write them in an Idea-Support Map like the one shown below.

2. Guide students to recognize what the important details have in common. Elicit from students that Sacagawea played an important role in an important expedition.

3. Work with students to write a main idea statement that describes what the selection is mostly about. Add the main idea statement to the Idea-Support Map.

> **MINILESSON PRINCIPLE**
>
> Readers look for important details in a text to figure out the main idea.

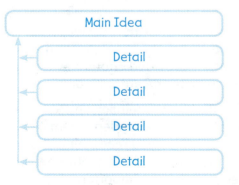

SUMMARIZE AND APPLY Restate the minilesson principle. Then tell students to apply it to their independent reading. Suggested language: "When you read, think about the important details the author gives to help you figure out the main idea."

GROUP SHARE Ask students to share a main idea from a book they read. Then have them name details that helped them figure it out.

78 • Lesson 20

Lesson 20

▶ Race Against Death

INTERACTIVE READ-ALOUD/SHARED READING

Read aloud the selection to students. Stop periodically for brief discussion of the text. Use the following suggested stopping points and prompts:

- After reading the first paragraph, ask: "How do you know this is a true story?" *(The author includes dates and quotes.)*
- After reading the first page, ask: "Why do you think the author calls the relay a race against death? Turn and talk about your thinking with a partner."
- At the end of the selection, ask: "What words and phrases does the author use to help you understand the dangers the sled dog teams faced on their journey?"

MINILESSON Genre: Narrative Nonfiction

TEACH Display the minilesson principle on chart paper, and read it aloud to students. Explain that authors share information in different ways to make information interesting. Explain that narrative nonfiction has some of the characteristics of a story, but it is about real people, events, and places.

1. Discuss the principle with students, using examples from *Race Against Death*. Suggested language: "One characteristic of a story is that the author uses a technique called suspense. Suspense is when the author gets the reader excited about learning the outcome of the events."

> **MINILESSON PRINCIPLE**
>
> Readers think about how the author shares information to make it interesting.

2. Ask students to explain how the author of *Race Against Death* used suspense. Elicit from students that the author revealed the events to readers just as they happened. Readers had to wait to find out whether the medicine would arrive in time, just as the people who experienced the events.

3. Have students explain how the characteristics of narrative nonfiction are similar to and different from other informational texts. Have them turn and talk to a partner about whether they enjoy reading about real people, events, and places in the form of a story.

SUMMARIZE AND APPLY Restate the minilesson principle. Tell students to apply it to their independent reading. Suggested language: "When you read, think about techniques the author uses to make the information interesting."

GROUP SHARE Have students share an example from their reading that shows how the author made information interesting.

▶ Native American Nature Poetry

INTERACTIVE READ-ALOUD/SHARED READING

Read aloud the poems to students. Stop periodically for brief discussion of the text. Use the following suggested stopping points and prompts:

- After reading the first poem, ask: "How does this poem make you feel about the moon? Turn and talk about your thinking with a partner."
- After reading the information about cylinder recorders, ask: "Why does the author include this information?" *(to tell the reader that it was an important tool Native Americans used to preserve their stories)*
- After reading the last poem, say: "Poems can make you feel different things such as sad, hopeful, lazy, or scared. Which of these poems gives you the strongest feeling? Tell a partner how it makes you feel."

MINILESSON Genre: Poetry

TEACH Display the minilesson principle on chart paper, and read it aloud to students. Explain to students that they are going to learn how the words in poems can help them create images in their minds.

1. Remind students that poets choose words for a poem very carefully so that readers will understand the precise meaning that the poet wants to share.

> **MINILESSON PRINCIPLE**
>
> Readers notice how poets use words to create images in readers' minds.

2. Read aloud "The Wind" to students again. Then ask: "What words in this poem help you visualize the wind?" Follow-up: "What does the wind look like? What does it sound like? How does the wind feel?" Tell students to answer the questions based on the image they have in their mind after reading the poem.

3. Next, ask a volunteer to read aloud the Nootka poem. Then have students explain what they see in their mind when they listen to the poem.

4. Guide students to recognize that if they replaced one or more words in the poem, its imagery and meaning would change. Work with students to replace the words *beautiful* and *rainbow* to create a different image in readers' minds.

SUMMARIZE AND APPLY Restate the minilesson principle. Tell students to apply it to their independent reading. Suggested language: "When you read a poem, think about the words the poet uses to help you create images in your mind."

GROUP SHARE Ask students to share a poem they read. Have them point out words in the poem that helped them create images in their mind.

Whole-Group Lessons • **79**

Whole-Group Lessons

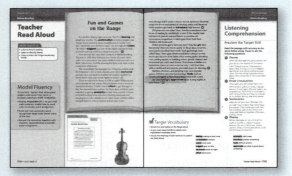

The World According to Humphrey
Student Book, Lesson 21

Fun and Games on the Range
Teacher's Edition, Lesson 21

Make the Switch
Student Book, Lesson 21

▶ The World According to Humphrey

INTERACTIVE READ-ALOUD/SHARED READING

Read aloud the story to students. Stop periodically for very brief discussion of the text. Use the following suggested stopping points and prompts for quick group response, or give a specific prompt and have partners or threes turn and talk.

- After A. J. introduces Humphrey, ask: "Who is telling this story?" (*Humphrey the hamster*)
- After the Thomases talk about breakfast, ask: "Why does the author use all capital letters for the conversation the Thomases are having?" (*to let readers know that they are talking very loudly*) Follow-up: "What has Humphrey noticed about the Thomases?"
- After Humphrey pulls out the plug, ask: "How does Humphrey feel about TV?" Follow-up: "How do you think the family will respond to Humphrey's Big Idea?"
- At the end of the story, say: "A. J.'s parents have changed. How do they feel about TV now? Turn and talk with a partner about why you think they feel this way now."

MINILESSON Theme

TEACH Display the minilesson principle on chart paper, and read it aloud to students. Tell students that they are going to think about how the lesson that characters learn in a story can help them determine the theme, or what the author is really trying to say to readers.

1. Discuss the principle with students, using examples from *The World According to Humphrey*. Focus on how the Thomas family changes when the TV goes off. Suggested language: "After Humphrey pulls out the plug, the Thomas family learns that there are a lot of fun things to do besides watching TV. How would you describe the lesson they learned?"

2. Guide students to understand the theme of the story. Suggested language: "The theme of a story is what the author is really trying to say to readers. What is the author really trying to say to readers by sharing this lesson about watching TV?" (*that people shouldn't watch so much TV*) Have students turn and talk with a partner about whether they agree with the author.

3. Explain to students that readers can interpret the theme of a story in different ways. Ask volunteers to explain how they would describe the theme in a way that makes it personal to them.

> **MINILESSON PRINCIPLE**
>
> Readers think about the lesson in the story to understand the theme, or what the author is really trying to say.

SUMMARIZE AND APPLY Restate the minilesson principle. Then tell students to apply it to their independent reading. Suggested language: "When you read a story, think about the lesson the author teaches to understand the theme."

GROUP SHARE Ask students to tell about a lesson the characters learned in a story they read. Have them explain how the lesson helped them understand the story's theme.

80 • Lesson 21

Lesson 21

▶ Fun and Games on the Range

INTERACTIVE READ-ALOUD/SHARED READING

Read aloud the selection to students. Stop periodically for brief discussion of the text. Use the following suggested stopping points and prompts:

- After reading about the sounds of life in 1850, say: "Compare your life at home with the lives of children in 1850. Turn and talk with a partner about how it is the same and how it is different."
- After reading about how pioneers had fun, ask: "Why do you think pioneers combined work and having fun?" Follow-up: "Which of these activities would you like to do?"
- At the end of the selection, ask: "How did the author of this selection organize information?"

MINILESSON Genre: Informational Text

TEACH Display the minilesson principle on chart paper, and read it aloud to students. Tell students that authors use interesting words and examples to get readers' attention.

1. Focus on the first paragraph of *Fun and Games on the Range*. Guide students to understand that the author grabs their attention with an interesting beginning. Suggested language: "The author describes a scene right at the beginning to get your attention and to make you feel like you are experiencing the sights and sounds. What interesting words does the author use?" (*TV is blaring, jangles your nerves, cuts through the racket*)

> **MINILESSON PRINCIPLE**
>
> Readers notice how the author uses words and interesting examples to get their attention.

2. Next, reread the paragraph about how pioneers relaxed. Point out to students that the author begins with a question to draw readers in to the paragraph and so that they will read on to answer it. Have students recall examples of relaxing activities that answer the question.

3. Ask students to think about the two techniques—using questions and making readers feel like they are part of the scene. Have them turn and talk with a partner about which technique they think is more effective in getting readers' attention.

SUMMARIZE AND APPLY Restate the minilesson principle. Tell students to apply it to their independent reading. Suggested language: "When you read, think about how the author uses words and interesting examples to get your attention."

GROUP SHARE Have students tell about words and interesting examples that got their attention when they read a story.

▶ Make the Switch

INTERACTIVE READ-ALOUD/SHARED READING

Read aloud the selection to students. Stop periodically for brief discussion of the text. Use the following suggested stopping points and prompts:

- After reading the introduction, ask: "What is the author saying about ads and how they try to influence you?" Follow-up: "What do you expect to see as you continue reading?"
- After reading the posters, ask: "How do the arrows and text help give you information?" (*They show some of the persuasive techniques used in ads.*)
- After reading the selection, say: "The author ends the selection by challenging you. Turn and talk with a partner. Explain what you think about the positive and negative effects of the posters."

MINILESSON Persuasion

TEACH Display the minilesson principle on chart paper, and read it aloud to students. Tell students that they are going to learn how authors use words and visuals to try to persuade them.

1. Guide students to understand the principle by focusing on the first poster in *Make the Switch*. Read the title aloud and ask: "How does the author want a reader to feel after reading the title?" Elicit from students that it makes sitting and watching the TV seem like a lazy thing to do.

> **MINILESSON PRINCIPLE**
>
> Readers notice how the author uses words and visuals to try to persuade them.

2. Focus on the visuals. Ask: "How does the boy look as he watches TV? How do you think he feels about the TV character? Turn and talk with a partner about how the author wants you to feel about watching TV."

3. Discuss the other poster with students. Have them point out how the words and visuals are used to persuade readers that the activities shown are a lot more fun to do than watching TV.

4. Have students share their ideas about which poster is more persuasive.

SUMMARIZE AND APPLY Restate the minilesson principle. Tell students to apply it to their independent reading. Suggested language: "When you read an ad or poster, think about how the author uses words and visuals to persuade you to think or act in a certain way."

GROUP SHARE Ask students to tell about an ad or poster they have read. Have them tell how the words and visuals try to persuade them to do something or think in a certain way.

Whole-Group Lessons • 81

Whole-Group Lessons

I Could Do That! Esther Morris Gets Women the Vote
Student Book, Lesson 22

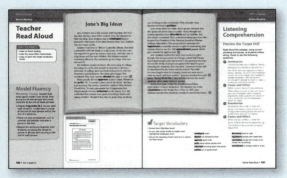

Jane's Big Ideas
Teacher's Edition, Lesson 22

Working for the Vote
Student Book, Lesson 22

▶ I Could Do That!

INTERACTIVE READ-ALOUD/SHARED READING

Read aloud the biography to students. Stop periodically for very brief discussion of the text. Use the following suggested stopping points and prompts for quick group response, or give a specific prompt and have partners or threes turn and talk.

- After Esther opens a hat shop, ask: "What kind of person do you think Esther was?" Follow-up: "What makes you think that?"
- After Esther moves to Illinois, say: "What pattern are you starting to see about what happened when people told Esther that she could not do something?"
- After women win the right to vote in Wyoming, ask: "How did Esther persuade the candidates to introduce a bill to allow women to vote?" *(She got everyone to agree that people in Wyoming were not afraid to try new things.)*
- At the end of the selection, ask: "How do you think Esther felt when she cast her first vote in Wyoming? Turn and talk about your thinking with a partner."

MINILESSON Cause and Effect

TEACH Display the minilesson principle on chart paper, and read it aloud to students. Remind students that a cause makes something else happen and that an effect is the result of a cause. Then tell students that they are going to learn to notice how many events can lead to one effect.

1. Discuss the principle with students, using cause-and-effect relationships in *I Could Do That!* Draw an Inference Map on chart paper, and write the following sentence in the bottom box: *In 1870, women in Wyoming voted for the first time.* Label the box *Effect*.

2. Then challenge readers to ask the question, "Why did this happen?" Tell students that when they think about why something happened, they are thinking about the cause of an event.

3. As students share their ideas about the causes for the event, write their responses in the Inference Map. Guide students to recognize that there were several causes that led to the effect.

> **MINILESSON PRINCIPLE**
>
> Readers notice how many events can lead to one effect.

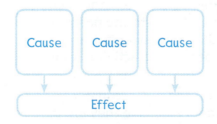

SUMMARIZE AND APPLY Restate the minilesson principle. Then tell students to apply it to their independent reading. Suggested language: "When you read, think about how many events can lead to one effect, or result."

GROUP SHARE Ask students to tell about causes and effects in a book they read. Have them explain several events that led to one effect.

82 • Lesson 22

Lesson 22

▶ Jane's Big Ideas

INTERACTIVE READ-ALOUD/SHARED READING

Read aloud the biography to students. Stop periodically for brief discussion of the text. Use the following suggested stopping points and prompts:

- After reading the first paragraph, ask: "What do you think the author means by saying that Jane Addams had big ideas?"
- After reading about Jane's pamphlet, ask: "What was Jane's reason for writing this pamphlet? Turn and talk about your thinking with a partner."
- At the end of the selection, ask: "Why do you think the author calls Jane a *tough cookie*?" Have students use examples from the selection to support their answers.

MINILESSON Cause and Effect

TEACH Display the minilesson principle on chart paper, and read it aloud to students. Remind them that a cause makes something else happen. The effect is the result of a cause. Then tell students that a cause can be a person's ideas. What the person does as a result of the ideas is the effect.

1. Discuss the principle with students, using examples from *Jane's Big Ideas*. Suggested language: "Jane Addams felt strongly about what women should be able to do. What were her big ideas?" After students summarize Jane's feelings about women's right to vote, tell students that her big ideas became the cause for change.

> **MINILESSON PRINCIPLE**
>
> Readers notice how a person's big ideas can cause changes for many people.

2. Next, ask students to think about the effects of Jane's big ideas. Suggested language: "Let's think about the result of Jane's big ideas. How did her ideas change life for many people?" Elicit from students that Jane challenged people to think about why women's ideas would be valuable in politics, and she influenced many people to change their views. Students should recognize that the 19th amendment was passed partly as a result of Jane's ideas.

SUMMARIZE AND APPLY Restate the minilesson principle. Tell students to apply it to their independent reading. Suggested language: "When you read a story, think about how a person's ideas cause changes in other people's lives."

GROUP SHARE Ask students to describe a person they read about. Have them tell how the person's ideas caused changes in other people's lives.

▶ Working for the Vote

INTERACTIVE READ-ALOUD/SHARED READING

Read aloud the play to students. Stop periodically for brief discussion of the text. Use the following suggested stopping points and prompts:

- After reading the first page, say: "The events in this play happened a long time ago. What can you tell so far about what life was like in 1851?"
- After Susan sees that Harriot is behind the door, ask: "Why do you think Harriot is interested in the conversation between Susan and Elizabeth?"
- At the end of the play, ask: "Why do you think Harriot finally got her chance to vote? Turn and talk about your thinking with a partner."

MINILESSON Genre: Play

TEACH Tell students that each character in a play has a role in telling the story. Explain that most of the characters are people who interact with one another. However, the narrator has a specific role that is different from all the other characters.

1. Use *Working for the Vote* to discuss the narrator's role in a play. Read aloud the narrator's first speaking part again. Then ask students to explain what they learned from it.

> **MINILESSON PRINCIPLE**
>
> Readers notice that the narrator of a play helps to move the story forward.

2. Summarize students' responses. Suggested language: "The narrator can tell background information about the characters and when the story takes place."

3. Then draw students' attention to the narrator's next two lines. Ask students to read them and to explain why they are important. Then summarize their responses. Suggested language: "The narrator helps you know important things about the story that the characters in the play do not say. The narrator can also explain some of the action."

4. Have students help you explain the narrator's role in a play as you write the minilesson principle on chart paper.

SUMMARIZE AND APPLY Restate the minilesson principle. Tell students to apply it to their independent reading. Suggested language: "When you read a play, notice how the narrator helps move the story forward."

GROUP SHARE Ask students to tell about a play they read. Have them explain the narrator's role and how the narrator helped move the story forward.

Whole-Group Lessons • **83**

Whole-Group Lessons

The Ever-Living Tree: The Life and Times of a Coast Redwood
Student Book, Lesson 23

Deserts on the Move?
Teacher's Edition, Lesson 23

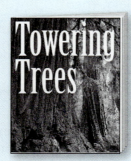

Towering Trees
Student Book, Lesson 23

▶ The Ever-Living Tree

INTERACTIVE READ-ALOUD/SHARED READING

Read aloud the selection to students. Stop periodically for very brief discussion of the text. Use the following suggested stopping points and prompts for quick group response, or give a specific prompt and have partners or threes turn and talk.

- After reading the first page, ask: "What kind of selection is this?" Follow-up: "What is the author telling you about?"
- After reading the second page, say: "The author did something interesting here by telling you about some events happening on the other side of the world. Why do you think she did this in a selection about a tree?"
- After reading about the Native Americans, ask: "Now that we've read several pages, what pattern do you see with how the author has organized information?"
- After reading about man walking on the moon, ask: "Why do you think the author included this information about space travel? Turn and talk about your ideas with a partner."
- At the end of the selection, ask: "Why do you think the author wrote this? How does it make you feel about the sequoia tree?"

MINILESSON Text and Graphic Features

TEACH Display the minilesson principle on chart paper, and read it aloud to students. Tell students that they are going to learn about why an author uses visuals such as diagrams, symbols, and timelines to help them understand the topic.

1. Discuss the principle, using examples from the first two pages of *The Ever-Living Tree*. Suggested language: "Look at the timeline in the top left corner of the page. Now look at the symbols at the beginning of each paragraph. What do you notice?" *(The symbols are the same.)* Tell students that the timeline shows the year when the tree started to grow and important events that happened later. Guide students to page through the selection to see how the timeline grows as the tree grows and time passes in history.

   > **MINILESSON PRINCIPLE**
   > Readers notice how visuals are related to a text and why the author used them.

2. Ask students to explain whether they think the author's choice to include a timeline and symbols helps them understand information about the sequoia.
3. Guide students to explain how other visuals in the selection support and relate to the main text. Draw their attention to the map, the diagram, and the illustrations.
4. Record students' responses in a T-Map like the one shown here. Have them explain how each visual connects to the ideas in the text.

Visual	What It Explains

SUMMARIZE AND APPLY Restate the minilesson principle. Then tell students to apply it to their independent reading. Suggested language: "When you read a selection, think about why the author used certain visuals to help you understand the topic."

GROUP SHARE Ask students to share what they learned from a visual in a book they read. Have them explain how the author used the visual, how it relates to the text, and how it helped them understand the topic.

84 • Lesson 23

Lesson 23

▶ Deserts on the Move?

INTERACTIVE READ-ALOUD/SHARED READING

Read aloud the selection to students. Stop periodically for brief discussion of the text. Use the following suggested stopping points and prompts:

- After reading the section Creeping Sands, ask: "How does the author make the information about deserts interesting?" *(by explaining how the land and people's lives change at the same time as the deserts change)*
- At the end of the selection, ask: "What does the author mean by saying that humans create the problem and also help to solve it? Turn and talk about your thinking with a partner."

MINILESSON Cause and Effect

TEACH Display the minilesson principle on chart paper, and read it aloud to students. Remind students that some events cause other events to happen. The first event that happens is the cause. The effect is what happens as a result. Tell students that they will learn to notice the language an author uses to explain causes and effects.

1. Discuss the principle, using examples from *Deserts on the Move?* Reread paragraph four aloud to students. Then say: "One way that authors show causes and effects is by using clue words such as *because, if, so,* and *when*." Reread the two sentences that begin with *If* to help students recognize the cause-and-effect relationships.

> **MINILESSON PRINCIPLE**
>
> Readers notice the language the author uses to explain causes and effects.

2. Write the causes and effects in a T-Map to illustrate the relationships.

3. Work with students to identify other causes and effects in the selection as you reread selected sentences. Have students indicate when the author used a clue word to help them understand causes and effects.

SUMMARIZE AND APPLY Restate the minilesson principle. Tell students to apply it to their independent reading. Suggested language: "When you read, think about the words the author uses to explain causes and effects."

GROUP SHARE Ask students to share a cause and an effect from a book they read. Have them give examples of words the author used to explain that cause and effect.

▶ Towering Trees

INTERACTIVE READ-ALOUD/SHARED READING

Read aloud the poems to students. Stop periodically for brief discussion of the text. Use the following suggested stopping points and prompts:

- After reading the introduction and "Ancestors of Tomorrow," ask: "How do the ideas in this poem relate to the topic of ancestors?" *(Ancestors are people who came before you. The poet compares people and their ancestors to trees and their branches and seeds.)* Follow-up: "What do you think about this comparison?"
- After reading about the Eon Tree, ask: "How does this poem tell a story? Turn and talk about your ideas with a partner."
- After reading the last poem, ask: "How does the poet help you picture the sequoia? What words and phrases does he use?"

MINILESSON Genre: Poetry

TEACH Display the minilesson principle on chart paper, and read it aloud to students. Explain to students that they are going to learn to recognize that poets can express ideas about a topic such as trees in different ways.

1. Discuss the principle, using examples from *Towering Trees*. Suggested language: "The three poems are about trees. Each poet expresses ideas about the trees in different ways. What do the trees in all the poems have in common?" *(They are all very old.)*

> **MINILESSON PRINCIPLE**
>
> Readers notice how poets can express ideas about the same topic in very different ways.

2. Next, point out the differences in the poems, including their structure and the feeling each poem gives the reader. Suggested language: "What is different about the ways the poems look?" Follow-up with questions that help students explain the mood and tone of the poems. Have students explain their answers to each question. Suggested language: "Which poem ends with a feeling of hope? Which poem makes the tree sound majestic? Which poem gives you a feeling of comfort?"

3. Have volunteers tell how they might approach writing a poem about a tree and how their poems would be different from the ones they read.

SUMMARIZE AND APPLY Restate the minilesson principle. Tell students to apply it to their independent reading. Suggested language: "When you read a poem, think about the unique way that the poet expresses ideas about a topic."

GROUP SHARE Ask students to share part of a poem they read. Have them point out words and techniques the poet used to make ideas about the topic unique.

Whole-Group Lessons • 85

Whole-Group Lessons

Owen and Mzee: The True Story of a Remarkable Friendship
Student Book, Lesson 24

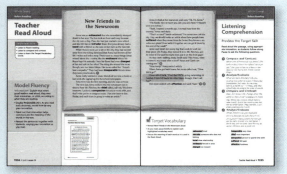

New Friends in the Newsroom
Teacher's Edition, Lesson 24

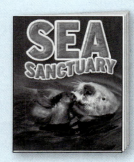

Sea Sanctuary
Student Book, Lesson 24

▶ Owen and Mzee

INTERACTIVE READ-ALOUD/SHARED READING

Read aloud the selection to students. Stop periodically for very brief discussion of the text. Use the following suggested stopping points and prompts for quick group response, or give a specific prompt and have partners or threes turn and talk.

- After reading the first page, ask: "Why was Haller Park a good place for Owen to go?"
- After the introduction to Mzee, ask: "What do you predict will happen with Mzee and Owen?"
- After reading that Owen would feed beside Mzee, ask: "Why do you think Owen felt safe with Mzee?"
- At the end of the selection, say: "The author gives a lot of reasons for why Owen and Mzee may have bonded. Which reasons do you think are correct? Turn and talk about your ideas with a partner."

MINILESSON Compare and Contrast

TEACH Display the minilesson principle on chart paper, and read it aloud to students. Remind students that comparing is telling how two things are alike and that contrasting is telling how two things are different. Tell students that comparing and contrasting ideas in a text can help them understand it better.

1. Discuss the principle with students, using examples from *Owen and Mzee*. Suggested language: "This selection tells about two unlikely friends. The reason their friendship is so surprising is because they are two very different animals. How are Owen and Mzee different?"
2. As students answer the question, write their responses on chart paper in a Venn Diagram.
3. Next, ask students to explain how the two animals are alike. Tell students to think about where they live, their friendship, and how they treat each other. Add students' responses to the Venn Diagram.

> **MINILESSON PRINCIPLE**
>
> Readers compare and contrast ideas to understand how things are alike and different.

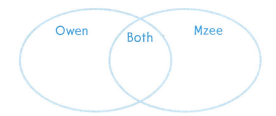

SUMMARIZE AND APPLY Restate the minilesson principle. Then tell students to apply it to their independent reading. Suggested language: "When you read, compare and contrast ideas to understand how things are alike and different."

GROUP SHARE Ask students to share two ideas from a book they have read. Have them explain how they are alike and different.

86 • Lesson 24

Lesson 24

▶ New Friends in the Newsroom

INTERACTIVE READ-ALOUD/SHARED READING

Read aloud the story to students. Stop periodically for brief discussion of the text. Use the following suggested stopping points and prompts:

- After reading the first two paragraphs, ask: "Why will Anna have a hard time finding things from her old home in the place where she lives now?"
- At the end of the story, ask: "How did Sarah make Anna comfortable in the city?" Follow-up: "How do you think writing the article helped Anna? Turn and talk about your ideas with a partner."

MINILESSON Genre: Realistic Fiction

TEACH Display the minilesson principle on chart paper, and read it aloud to students. Tell students that the setting of a story can be as important as the characters. Explain that looking for the author's description of the setting will help them understand when and where the story takes place and also how it affects the characters.

1. Discuss the principle with students, using examples from *New Friends in the Newsroom*. Focus on the first paragraph. Suggested language: "The author says that Anna just started a new school and that she has to ride a bus for an hour because the city is so big. This tells you that the story takes place at a school in a city."

> **MINILESSON PRINCIPLE**
>
> Readers look for the author's description of the setting to understand when and where the story takes place.

2. Focus on other details in the story that describe when the story takes place. Ask: "Does this story take place now or long ago?" *(now)* "How does the author let you know this?" Have students give details from the story to support their answers. Then ask students to talk with a partner about why the setting of the story is important.

SUMMARIZE AND APPLY Restate the minilesson principle. Tell students to apply it to their independent reading. Suggested language: "When you read, look for the author's description of the setting to understand where and when the story takes place. Think about how the setting affects the characters."

GROUP SHARE Ask students to share an example of how the author described the setting in a story they read. Have them explain why the setting was important.

▶ Sea Sanctuary

INTERACTIVE READ-ALOUD/SHARED READING

Read aloud the selection to students. Stop periodically for brief discussion of the text. Use the following suggested stopping points and prompts:

- After reading the first page, ask: "Based on the information the author has told you, what is a sanctuary?" Follow-up: "What is unique about the sanctuary that the author describes?"
- After reading the section Seafood Chain, ask: "How has the author organized the information in this section?" *(cause and effect)*
- After reading the section Flower Garden Banks, ask: "How is this sanctuary the same as or different from the Monterey Bay National Marine Sanctuary?"
- At the end of the selection, ask: "Why do you think sea sanctuaries are important? Turn and talk about your thinking with a partner."

MINILESSON Summarize

TEACH Display the minilesson principle on chart paper, and read it aloud to students. Tell students that summarizing a text in their own words is a strategy they can use to be sure they understand what they read.

1. Discuss the principle with students by using the selection *Sea Sanctuary*. Suggested language: "When you summarize, you explain the main ideas and the most important details of a text in your own words. Look at the first two pages of the selection. What is the main idea of these pages?" *(The Monterey Bay National Marine Sanctuary is an ecosystem where animals live and find good sources of food.)* Write students' correct responses on chart paper.

> **MINILESSON PRINCIPLE**
>
> Readers summarize a text in their own words to be sure they understand it.

2. Repeat the process for the second page.

3. Work with students to combine the main idea statements into a two- or three-sentence summary. *(Sea sanctuaries are places where marine animals live and thrive because they are protected. In Monterey Bay and Flower Garden Banks Sanctuaries, each animal is part of a food chain.)* Point out to students that the summary is much shorter than the complete text, and it does not include minor details.

SUMMARIZE AND APPLY Restate the minilesson principle. Tell students to apply it to their independent reading. Suggested language: "When you read, summarize the ideas in your own words to be sure you understand them."

GROUP SHARE Ask students to summarize a book they read. Remind them to tell about the ideas in their own words.

Whole-Group Lessons • **87**

Whole-Group Lessons

The Fun They Had
Student Book, Lesson 25

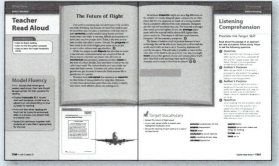

The Future of Flight
Teacher's Edition, Lesson 25

Technology for All Learners
Student Book, Lesson 25

▶ The Fun They Had

INTERACTIVE READ-ALOUD/SHARED READING

Read aloud the story to students. Stop periodically for very brief discussion of the text. Use the following suggested stopping points and prompts for quick group response, or give a specific prompt and have partners or threes turn and talk.

- After reading the first page, ask: "When does this story take place?" *(in the future)* Follow-up: "Besides the diary entry, how do you know that this is the future?"
- After the man fixes the mechanical teacher, ask: "How do you think the author wants you to feel about the mechanical teacher? Turn and talk with a partner about details that let you know."
- After Tommy walks away with the book, say: "Margie wants to read the old book some more. How do you think she feels about schools in the past?"
- At the end of the story, have students turn and talk with a partner about whether they would rather go to schools like we have today or schools in the future like the author describes. Have them use text evidence to explain their thinking.

MINILESSON Author's Purpose

TEACH Display the minilesson principle on chart paper, and read it aloud to students. Remind students that authors have different reasons for writing. Tell students that they are going to look for details that will help them figure out the author's reason for writing.

1. Discuss the principle with students, focusing on the author's use of humorous details in *The Fun They Had*. Suggested language: "The author included some funny details in the story he told about the future."

2. Work with students to identify humorous details in the story. Guide them to understand that the details were funny because of the characters' reactions to learning about what schools were like in the past. For example, they had never seen a book.

3. Write on the board the following purposes for writing: to inform, to entertain, to persuade. Ask students to explain the author's reason for writing *The Fun They Had*. Elicit from students that the humorous details indicate that the story was written to entertain readers.

> **MINILESSON PRINCIPLE**
>
> Readers look for details to figure out the author's reason for writing.

SUMMARIZE AND APPLY Restate the minilesson principle. Then tell students to apply it to their independent reading. Suggested language: "When you read, think about details that help you understand the author's reason for writing."

GROUP SHARE Ask students to tell about a story they read. Have them name details in the story that helped them figure out the author's reason for writing it.

Lesson 25

▶ The Future of Flight

INTERACTIVE READ-ALOUD/SHARED READING

Read aloud the selection to students. Stop periodically for brief discussion of the text. Use the following suggested stopping points and prompts:

- After the first paragraph, ask: "How do you think the author feels about flight? Turn and talk with a partner about your thinking."
- After the first page, ask: "What problems do airplanes cause?"
- At the end of the selection, ask: "Why do you think the author wrote this selection? Turn and talk about your thinking with a partner."

MINILESSON Genre: Informational Text

TEACH Display the minilesson principle on chart paper, and read it aloud to students. Explain to students that authors use evidence to explain why they think a topic is important. Tell students that it is their job to think about what the author writes and decide whether they agree.

1. Discuss the principle with students, using examples from *The Future of Flight*. Have students identify reasons the author gives to show that the field of flight is important. (*It is inexpensive compared with earlier types of travel, it's quicker, and it gives people access to other cultures and opportunities.*)

> **MINILESSON PRINCIPLE**
>
> Readers think about why the author feels the subject is important and decide whether they agree.

2. Next, have students explain other evidence the author gives to support the idea that flight is an ideal way to travel.

3. Explain to students that they may agree or disagree with an author's ideas. Tell them that they should evaluate the evidence to form their own opinions. Have students turn and talk with a partner about whether they think the subject of flight is important for people to learn about. Have them use evidence to explain their thinking.

SUMMARIZE AND APPLY Restate the minilesson principle. Tell students to apply it to their independent reading. Suggested language: "When you read, think about why the author feels the subject is important. Look at the evidence the author gives and decide whether you agree."

GROUP SHARE Have students share a book they read and tell why the author felt the subject was important. Then have them tell whether they agree and why.

▶ Technology for All Learners

INTERACTIVE READ-ALOUD/SHARED READING

Read aloud the selection to students. Stop periodically for brief discussion of the text. Use the following suggested stopping points and prompts:

- After the introduction, ask: "How does the author feel about students missing school?"
- After reading the section Meet PEBBLES, ask: "What information does the diagram give you?" (*It shows how the PEBBLES robot works.*)
- At the end of the selection, ask: "How does the author feel about technology?" Follow-up: "What do you think are some of the benefits and disadvantages of the technology she describes? Turn and talk with a partner about your thinking."

MINILESSON Summarize

TEACH Display the minilesson principle on chart paper, and read it aloud to students. Tell students that summarizing information can help them understand it.

1. Guide students to understand the principle by focusing on the first page of *Technology for All Learners*. Suggested language: "When you summarize, you tell about the main ideas and the important details that support the main ideas. What is the main idea of this page, or what is it mostly about?" (*Sick students miss many weeks of school.*) Have students point out details that support this main idea.

> **MINILESSON PRINCIPLE**
>
> Readers summarize information in their own words to be sure they understand it.

2. Focus on the next section of the selection. Suggested language: "What is the main idea of this section?" (*A robotic system called PEBBLES can help students.*) Follow-up: "What are some details that tell about how PEBBLES helps students?"

3. Repeat for the last section of the selection.

4. Work with students to combine all the main ideas into a two- or three-sentence summary of the selection. Remind students that they should use their own words in a summary.

SUMMARIZE AND APPLY Restate the minilesson principle. Tell students to apply it to their independent reading. Suggested language: "When you read, summarize the main ideas and details to be sure you understand the information."

GROUP SHARE Ask students to summarize part of a book they read. Remind them to include the main ideas and details in it.

Whole-Group Lessons • **89**

Whole-Group Lessons

The Girl Who Loved Spiders
Student Magazine, Lesson 26

Web Wise
Student Magazine, Lesson 26

Poetry Place: "The Spider" and "Spider Ropes"
Student Magazine, Lesson 26

▶ The Girl Who Loved Spiders

INTERACTIVE READ-ALOUD/SHARED READING

Read aloud the story to students. Stop periodically for very brief discussion of the text. Use the following suggested stopping points and prompts for quick group response, or give a specific prompt and have partners or threes turn and talk.

- After reading the first page, ask: "Who is telling this story?" (*a boy*) Follow-up: "How does this make the selection more interesting to read?"
- After reading the second page, ask: "How do you think Luis feels about moving to Florida? What does he say that makes you think this?"
- After Ashanti stalks away, ask: "Why does Ashanti stalk away?" (*She is still angry with Luis for surprising her and frustrated that he doesn't like spiders.*) Follow-up: "Turn and talk with a partner about how you think Luis feels about Ashanti."
- After Ashanti shows Luis the poster of Anansi, ask: "Do you think Luis and Ashanti will become friends? Turn and talk with a partner about your thinking."
- At the end of the selection, ask: "How does the author use photographs and captions in the story?" (*to show you what real spiders look like and to give facts that help you learn about them*)

MINILESSON Story Structure

TEACH Display the minilesson principle on chart paper, and read it aloud to students. Tell students that they are going to learn about the problem and solution in a story.

1. Explain to students that the characters in stories often have a problem to solve. Guide students to identify Luis's problem in *The Girl Who Loved Spiders*. Suggested language: "At the beginning of the story, you learned that Luis hates spiders. Why was this a problem for Luis?" (*He moved to Florida and there are all kinds of spiders there.*)

   MINILESSON PRINCIPLE
   Readers notice the problem in a story and how it is solved.

2. Talk with students about how Ashanti helped Luis solve his problem. Ask: "How did Luis feel about spiders at the end of the story?" (*He was not afraid of them anymore.*) Follow-up: "How do you know?" (*He said they are kind of cool, and he wanted to know what kinds of spiders were in his yard.*)

3. Record students' ideas about the problem and solution in a Story Map like the one shown here.

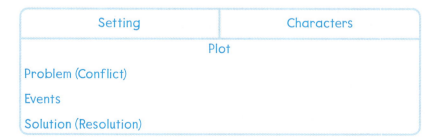

SUMMARIZE AND APPLY Restate the minilesson principle. Tell students to look for a problem and solution in their reading. Suggested language: "When you read, think about what problem the characters have. Then think about how the problem was solved."

GROUP SHARE Ask students to share a problem from a story they read. Then have them tell how the problem was solved.

90 • Lesson 26

Lesson 26

▶ Web Wise

INTERACTIVE READ-ALOUD/SHARED READING

Read aloud the selection to students. Stop periodically for brief discussion of the text. Use the following suggested stopping points and prompts:

- After reading the introduction, ask: "What will you learn about in this selection?" (*spider webs*) Follow-up: "How does the author feel about spiders? How do you know?"
- After reading the section Web Shots, ask: "Why do you think scientists and photographers want to take pictures of spider webs? Turn and talk with a partner about your thinking."
- After reading the section Strange, but True!, ask: "Do you think spiders are intelligent? What did you learn from this selection that makes you think that way?"

MINILESSON Genre: Informational Text

TEACH Display the minilesson principle on chart paper, and read it aloud to students. Remind students that *Web Wise* is an informational text—it tells facts about a topic. Tell students that they are going to use features in the text to help them locate information.

1. Discuss the principle with students, using the introduction from *Web Wise* as an example. Point out the introduction. Suggested language: "At the beginning of the selection, the author wrote a short introduction. I read the introduction to find out what the selection is about."

> **MINILESSON PRINCIPLE**
> Readers use the features of informational text to locate information.

2. Next, point out the headings and read them aloud. Guide students to understand the purpose of headings. Suggested language: "The author used headings to organize the information. What section would you read to learn about how to photograph spider webs?" (*Web Shots*)

3. Finally, talk with students about how the author used photos in the selection. Ask: "Why did the author use photos in the selection?" (*to help readers better understand the information in each section*)

SUMMARIZE AND APPLY Restate the minilesson principle. Tell students to apply it to their independent reading. Suggested language: "When you read an informational text, look for special features that can help you locate different kinds of information."

GROUP SHARE Have students share an informational text from their reading. Have them name the features in the text and tell how those features helped them locate information.

▶ Poetry Place

INTERACTIVE READ-ALOUD/SHARED READING

Read aloud the poems to students. Stop periodically for brief discussion of them. Use the following suggested stopping points and prompts:

- After reading "The Spider," ask: "What is this poem about?" (*how a spider captures its prey*) Follow-up: "How does the poet make this information interesting?" (*The poet uses interesting adjectives to describe the spider and its web.*)
- After reading "Spider Ropes," ask: "What does this poem tell about?" (*It tells about a child who goes exploring in the woods.*) Follow-up: "Explain whether you think 'Spider Ropes' is a good name for this poem. Turn and talk with a partner about your thinking."

MINILESSON Genre: Poetry

TEACH Display the minilesson principle on chart paper, and read it aloud to students. Tell students they will learn to look for clues in poems that help them understand their meaning.

1. Guide students to understand the principle by focusing on "The Spider." Suggested language: "This poem doesn't say what the spider will do with the flies. What do you think the spider will do?" (*eat the flies*) Follow-up: "What clues does the poet give to make you think that?" (*The poet says the spider is sly and that she won't apologize for the flies getting stuck in the web.*)

> **MINILESSON PRINCIPLE**
> Readers look for clues to understand a poem's meaning.

2. Read "Spider Ropes" aloud. Then ask: "What does this poem tell about?" (*a walk in the woods*) Follow-up: "What clues does the poet give to help you understand its meaning?" (*The poet tells about things you can come across, such as leaves and spiders' webs, when exploring in the woods.*)

SUMMARIZE AND APPLY Restate the minilesson principle. Tell students to apply it to their independent reading. Suggested language: "When you read a poem, look for clues that help you understand its meaning."

GROUP SHARE Ask students to share a poem they read. Have them point out the clues in the poem that helped them understand its meaning.

Whole-Group Lessons • 91

Whole-Group Lessons

▶ Amphibian Alert!

INTERACTIVE READ-ALOUD/SHARED READING

Read aloud the selection to students. Stop periodically for very brief discussion of the text. Use the following suggested stopping points and prompts for quick group response, or give a specific prompt and have partners or threes turn and talk.

- After reading the first page, say: "What kind of information does the author give about amphibians?"
- After reading the first two pages, ask: "How do you think the author feels about amphibians?" Follow-up: "What does the author say to make you think that?"
- After reading the section Introduced Species and Fungus, say: "The author tells about some things that are a threat to the lives of amphibians. Turn and talk with a partner about which threat you think is the most serious and why."
- At the end of the selection, ask: "How does the author organize the information in the selection?" Follow-up: "How does this help you understand the information?"

Amphibian Alert!
Student Magazine, Lesson 27

MINILESSON Main Ideas and Details

TEACH Display the minilesson principle on chart paper, and read it aloud to students. Tell students that authors often state the main idea of a paragraph in the first or last sentence. Then explain that in some cases, authors do not state the main idea at all, but they expect readers to figure it out using details provided.

1. Discuss the principle with students, using examples from *Amphibian Alert!* Focus on the section Habitat Loss and Pollution. Tell students that the main idea of this section is not stated. Suggested language: "The author doesn't directly state the main idea of this section. You have to think about the details in the section and figure out the main idea. The main idea of this paragraph is *Loss of habitat and water pollution are two things that threaten the lives of amphibians.*" Have students name details the author gives that tell about this main idea.

   > **MINILESSON PRINCIPLE**
   > Readers notice that the main idea can be stated or unstated.

2. Next, focus on the section Plans to Help. Guide students to understand that the main idea of this section is stated in the first sentence: *Scientists and conservation groups from around the world are putting plans together to help save amphibians.* Have students name details in the section that tell about this main idea.

3. Work with students to state the main idea of other sections in the selection. Have them name details that tell about the main idea. Record their responses in an Idea-Support Map like the one shown here.

The Frog in the Milk Pail
Student Magazine, Lesson 27

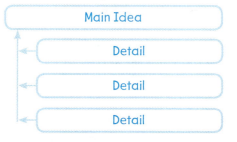

Main Idea
Detail
Detail
Detail

Poetry Place: "Toad by the Road" and "The Poison-Dart Frogs"
Student Magazine, Lesson 27

SUMMARIZE AND APPLY Restate the minilesson principle. Tell students to apply it to their independent reading. Suggested language: "When you read, think about whether the author states the main idea or expects you to figure it out."

GROUP SHARE Have students name a main idea from a book they read. Have them tell whether the main idea was stated or unstated.

92 • Lesson 27

Lesson 27

▶ The Frog in the Milk Pail

INTERACTIVE READ-ALOUD/SHARED READING

Read aloud the fable to students. Stop periodically for brief discussion of the text. Use the following suggested stopping points and prompts:

- After reading the first page, say: "The frog is curious and determined. Give examples from the story that help you know this." (*The frog tastes new things he comes upon as he goes exploring. The frog does not let any difficulties that come his way discourage him.*)
- After reading the section The Science of Butter, ask: "Why do you think the author includes this information? Turn and talk about your thinking with a partner."

MINILESSON Genre: Fable

TEACH Display the minilesson principle on chart paper, and read it aloud to students. Tell students you are going to think about how a character's actions are used to explain a lesson or moral in a fable.

1. Remind students that fables are written to teach readers a lesson about life. Explain that thinking about what the characters do in a fable can help them understand the lesson. Suggested language: "In the fable *The Frog in the Milk Pail*, the frog kept hopping along and exploring no matter what happened to him. How did not giving up help the frog?" (*The frog was able to get out from being stuck in the milk pail.*)

> **MINILESSON PRINCIPLE**
> Readers notice how characters' actions are used to explain a lesson or moral.

2. Tell students that the author included other details to help explain the lesson. Guide them to identify details about the frog's actions that support the lesson that you should never give up.

SUMMARIZE AND APPLY Restate the minilesson principle. Tell students to apply it to their independent reading. Suggested language: "When you read a fable, think about how the characters' actions help to explain the lesson or moral of the story."

GROUP SHARE Have students share a lesson they learned in their reading. Tell them to explain how the characters' actions in the story helped explain the lesson.

▶ Poetry Place

INTERACTIVE READ-ALOUD/SHARED READING

Read aloud the poems to students. Stop periodically for brief discussion of the text. Use the following suggested stopping points and prompts:

- After reading "Toad by the Road," ask: "What does this poem tell you about what toads are like?" (*that toads like to be still and like to sing*) Follow-up: "How does the rhyme in the poem make it more interesting to read?"
- After reading "The Poison-Dart Frogs," ask: "What does the author mean by saying that the frogs are 'Masters of Fine Art'?" (*The author thinks the frogs' colors are as beautiful as fine art.*) Follow-up: "How does the author describe each frog?"

MINILESSON Genre: Poetry

TEACH Display the minilesson principle on chart paper, and read it aloud to students. Have students name the five senses as you write them on chart paper. Tell them they will learn to notice how poets use strong verbs and adjectives to appeal to the readers' senses.

1. Discuss the principle with students, using examples from "Toad by the Road." Suggested language: "Poets often use more exciting verbs to make their writing lively and interesting. Strong verbs such as *hustle* and *hurry* help you see and feel what is happening better than verbs like *go* or *pass by* would."

> **MINILESSON PRINCIPLE**
> Readers notice how poets use strong verbs and adjectives to appeal to the senses.

2. Point out other verbs and adjectives the author uses, such as *wiggle*, *flicker*, *glorious*, and *savor*. Have students tell how these words make the poem more interesting.

3. Then read "The Poison-Dart Frogs" aloud. Ask: "What do you see and feel when you read this poem?" Follow-up: "What words does the poet use to make you see and feel those things?"

SUMMARIZE AND APPLY Restate the minilesson principle. Tell students to apply it to their independent reading. Suggested language: "When you read a poem, notice the words the poet uses to appeal to your senses."

GROUP SHARE Ask students to share a poem they read. Have them point out strong verbs and adjectives that appeal to their senses.

Whole-Group Lessons • 93

Whole-Group Lessons

Museums: Worlds of Wonder
Student Magazine, Lesson 28

Making the Most from Trash
Student Magazine, Lesson 28

Poetry Place: "Dinosaur Bone" and "Museum Farewell"
Student Magazine, Lesson 28

▶ Museums: Worlds of Wonder

INTERACTIVE READ-ALOUD/SHARED READING

Read aloud the selection to students. Stop periodically for very brief discussion of the text. Use the following suggested stopping points and prompts for quick group response, or give a specific prompt and have partners or threes turn and talk.

- After reading the first page, ask: "What information does the map give you?"
- After reading about the National Air and Space Museum, ask: "How does the author organize the information in the selection?"
- After reading about the Field Museum, ask: "What information does the photograph give you?" Have students turn and talk with a partner about how the photograph helps them understand more about the text.
- At the end of the selection, ask: "Which museum would you like to visit? Turn and talk with a partner about your choice."

MINILESSON Fact and Opinion

TEACH Display the minilesson principle on chart paper, and read it aloud to students. Remind them that facts tell true information that can be proved. The author's thoughts, feelings, or beliefs are opinions. Explain that it is important to notice the difference between facts and the author's opinions as they read because they can agree or disagree with opinions.

1. Discuss the principle with students, using examples from *Museums: Worlds of Wonder*. Suggested language: "The author states that museums are wonderful places. This statement is not a fact. It tells how the author feels about museums. The author also states that there are different kinds of museums. That is a fact. It gives information that can be proved."

2. Reread the section City Museum of St. Louis, Missouri. Have students identify a fact or an opinion. Suggested language: "The author said that *there's an amazing playground* at the museum. Is this a fact or an opinion?" (*opinion*) Follow-up: "How do you know?" (*It tells how the author feels about the playground. The idea can't be proved.*)

3. Explain to students that some words and phrases are clues that the author is stating a thought, feeling, or belief. Write the following examples on chart paper: *should, best, I think, believe*.

4. Elicit from students additional examples of facts and opinions. Record students' responses in a T-Map. Have volunteers tell whether they agree with the author's opinions and why.

> **MINILESSON PRINCIPLE**
>
> Readers notice the difference between facts and the author's thoughts, feelings, or beliefs.

Facts	Thoughts, Feelings, Beliefs

SUMMARIZE AND APPLY Restate the minilesson principle. Then tell students to apply it to their independent reading. Suggested language: "When you read, look for facts and what the author thinks, feels, or believes. Think about how you know the difference between facts and opinions."

GROUP SHARE Have students tell about a book they read. Ask them to share a fact that the author states and one of the author's thoughts, feelings, or beliefs. Have them explain how they know it is a fact or the author's opinion.

Lesson 28

▶ Making the Most from Trash

INTERACTIVE READ-ALOUD/SHARED READING

Read aloud the selection to students. Stop periodically for brief discussion of the text. Use the following suggested stopping points and prompts:

- After reading the introduction, ask: "How does the author feel about trash?" (*The author thinks the amount of trash people make is a problem.*)
- After reading the section Flakes to Fleece, ask: "How does the author organize information in this section?" (*in time order*)
- At the end of the selection, ask: "Why do you think the author wrote this selection? Turn and talk about your thinking with a partner."

MINILESSON Fact and Opinion

TEACH Display the minilesson principle on chart paper, and read it aloud to students. Tell students that authors often use facts to support their opinions. They give facts that explain how they formed that opinion.

1. Discuss the principle with students, using examples from *Making the Most from Trash*. Suggested language: "The author has the opinion that people can do something about the trash problem by reducing, reusing, and recycling. The author then gives facts about different ways this can be done."

> **MINILESSON PRINCIPLE**
> Readers notice how authors support opinions with facts.

2. Work with students to name the different facts that the author used to support the opinion that the trash problem can be solved. (*We can reduce the amount of things we use, reuse things instead of throwing them out, and recycle tires and different kinds of plastic.*)

3. Ask students to tell whether they agree with the author's opinion about trash. Suggested language: "Do you think the author included enough facts to support this opinion? Why or why not?"

SUMMARIZE AND APPLY Restate the minilesson principle. Tell students to apply it to their independent reading. Suggested language: "When you read, think about the author's opinion and the facts the author uses to support that opinion."

GROUP SHARE Ask students to name an opinion from a book they read. Have them tell facts the author provided to support that opinion.

▶ Poetry Place

INTERACTIVE READ-ALOUD/SHARED READING

Read aloud the poems to students. Stop periodically for brief discussion of the text. Use the following suggested stopping points and prompts:

- After reading "Dinosaur Bone," ask: "Where is the dinosaur bone?" (*in a museum*) Follow-up: "How does the illustration help you to know this?"
- After reading "Museum Farewell," ask: "What is this poem about?" (*closing time at a museum*) Follow-up: "How does the rhyme make the poem more interesting to read? Turn and talk with a partner about your thinking."

MINILESSON Genre: Poetry

TEACH Display the minilesson principle on chart paper, and read it aloud to students. Explain that poets choose words carefully to help readers feel a certain way.

1. Guide students to understand the principle by focusing on "Dinosaur Bone." Suggested language: "This poem told the thoughts someone had while looking at a dinosaur bone in a museum. Think about the words *secret* and *tell me* in the poem. What feeling do these words give you?" (*a feeling of mystery*)

> **MINILESSON PRINCIPLE**
> Readers think about the feeling the poem gives them.

2. Then focus on the questions in the poem. Ask: "The poet also used a lot of questions in the poem. How do the questions contribute to this feeling of mystery? Turn and talk about your thinking with a partner."

3. Next, reread "Museum Farewell." Ask: "How does this poem make you feel?" Guide students to recognize that words in the poem convey a feeling of peace and quiet.

SUMMARIZE AND APPLY Restate the minilesson principle. Tell students to apply it to their independent reading. Suggested language: "When you read a poem, think about the feeling the poem gives you."

GROUP SHARE Ask students to share a poem from their reading. Have them tell about the feeling the poem gives them.

Whole-Group Lessons • **95**

Whole-Group Lessons

Save Timber Woods!
Student Magazine, Lesson 29

John Muir: A Persuasive Essay
Student Magazine, Lesson 29

Poetry Place: "The Comb of Trees" and "Enjoy the Earth"
Student Magazine, Lesson 29

▶ Save Timber Woods!

INTERACTIVE READ-ALOUD/SHARED READING

Read aloud the play to students. Stop periodically for very brief discussion of the text. Use the following suggested stopping points and prompts for quick group response, or give a specific prompt and have partners or threes turn and talk.

- After previewing the play, ask: "How is a play different from a story?" (*A play is a story that can be performed for an audience.*) Follow-up: "Turn and talk with a partner about the features you find in a play."
- After the students find out that Timber Woods is going to be sold, ask: "Why don't the students want Timber Woods to be sold?" (*They will lose a place to camp and picnic; animals will lose their homes.*)
- After reading Scene II, ask: "What do the friends decide to do to persuade the town to buy Timber Woods?" (*They decide to go to the town council meeting and give reasons why the town should buy Timber Woods.*) Follow-up: "Do you think their idea will work? Turn and talk about your thinking with a partner."
- At the end of the play, ask: "Why do you think the author wrote this play?"

MINILESSON Understanding Characters

TEACH Display the minilesson principle on chart paper, and read it aloud to students. Explain to students that thinking about the things characters say and do can help them understand the reasons for their actions.

1. Discuss the principle with students, using Gina from *Save Timber Woods!* as an example. Suggested language: "Gina talks about the deer that are eating trees in her family's backyard. Saving backyards from the deer is the reason Gina wants to save Timber Woods."

2. Focus on another character in the play, such as Lucas. Suggested language: "Why does Lucas want to save Timber Woods?" (*Lucas wants to save animals' homes.*) Follow-up: "What does Lucas say and do to help you know that?"

3. Work with students to understand reasons for other characters' actions in the play. Record their ideas in a T-Map like the one shown here.

> **MINILESSON PRINCIPLE**
>
> Readers notice what characters say and do to understand the reasons for their actions.

Characters	Reasons

SUMMARIZE AND APPLY Restate the minilesson principle. Then tell students to apply it to their independent reading. Suggested language: "When you read, think about what the characters say and do. Think about how that helps you understand the reasons for their actions."

GROUP SHARE Ask students to tell about a character in a story they read. Have them give reasons for the character's actions.

Lesson 29

▶ John Muir

INTERACTIVE READ-ALOUD/SHARED READING

Read aloud the selection to students. Stop periodically for brief discussion of the text. Use the following suggested stopping points and prompts:

- After reading the first page, ask: "How did the walks John Muir took help him decide what to do with his life?"
- After reading about Yosemite, ask: "Why do you think the author tells you about Yosemite?"
- After reading the selection, ask: "Do you think protecting nature is important? Turn and talk about your thinking with a partner."

MINILESSON Persuasion

TEACH Display the minilesson principle on chart paper, and read it aloud to students. Explain to students that they are going to learn how authors use details in a selection to support their persuasive message.

1. Discuss the principle with students, using *John Muir: A Persuasive Essay*. Tell students that the author wanted to persuade readers about the importance of preserving nature. Explain that the author shared this message by using John Muir as an example. Suggested language: "The author wanted to persuade readers that John Muir set a good example for how people can protect nature. The author gave details about the things John Muir did to learn about the importance of nature."

> **MINILESSON PRINCIPLE**
>
> Readers look for support in a text to understand the author's persuasive message.

2. Discuss the example of how John Muir explored the outdoors. Ask: "What did John Muir learn as he explored the wilderness?" (*He learned all about rocks, plants, and animals.*) Follow-up: "Why was this important?" (*It helped him understand the importance of the wilderness.*)

3. Work with students to identify other things John Muir did to learn about the importance of nature. Ask: "Why does the author believe that John Muir is a good example to follow for people who want to protect nature?" Follow-up: "What details did she include to make you think that way?"

SUMMARIZE AND APPLY Restate the minilesson principle. Tell students to apply it to their independent reading. Suggested language: "When you read, look for details that support the author's message."

GROUP SHARE Have students tell about the author's message in a book they read. Have them give examples of details the author used to support his or her message.

▶ Poetry Place

INTERACTIVE READ-ALOUD/SHARED READING

Read aloud the poems to students. Stop periodically for brief discussion of the text. Use the following suggested stopping points and prompts:

- After reading "The Comb of Trees," ask: "Why does the poet compare the trees to a comb?" (*to help the reader visualize what the trees look like*) Follow-up: "How does the poet feel about the trees? What does the poet say to let you know that?"
- After reading "Enjoy the Earth," ask: "What does the poet mean by the phrase enjoy the earth gently?" (*The poet means that it is okay to enjoy what the earth has to offer, but that we should also take care of it.*) Follow-up: "Do you agree with the poet's message? Turn and talk with a partner about your thinking."

MINILESSON Genre: Poetry

TEACH Display the minilesson principle on chart paper, and read it aloud to students. Tell students that they are going to learn about how poets use language to help the reader see, feel, and hear what they are describing.

1. Tell students that poets use language in special ways that help readers share an experience or feeling. Read aloud "The Comb of Trees." Then ask: "What language did the poet use to help you visualize the trees?"

> **MINILESSON PRINCIPLE**
>
> Readers notice language that helps them see, feel, and hear what the poet describes.

2. Talk about other words or phrases the poet used to help the reader see, hear, or feel what the trees are like.

3. Next, read aloud "Enjoy the Earth." Then ask: "How does this poem make you feel? Turn and talk about your thinking with a partner."

4. Guide students to recognize that if they replaced one or more words in the poem, its imagery and meaning would change. Work with students to replace the words *enjoy* and *gently* to create a different image in readers' minds.

SUMMARIZE AND APPLY Restate the minilesson principle. Tell students to apply it to their independent reading. Suggested language: "When you read a poem, notice the language that helps you see, feel, and hear what the poet describes."

GROUP SHARE Ask students to share a poem from their reading. Have them point out words that help them see, feel, and hear what the poet describes.

Whole-Group Lessons • **97**

Whole-Group Lessons

Mystery at Reed's Pond
Student Magazine, Lesson 30

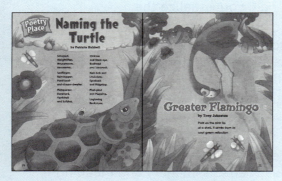

A Big Python Problem
Student Magazine, Lesson 30

Poetry Place: "Naming the Turtle" and "Greater Flamingo"
Student Magazine, Lesson 30

▶ Mystery at Reed's Pond

INTERACTIVE READ-ALOUD/SHARED READING

Read aloud the story to students. Stop periodically for very brief discussion of the text. Use the following suggested stopping points and prompts for quick group response, or give a specific prompt and have partners or threes turn and talk.

- After reading the first page, ask: "Where does the story take place?" (*at a pond*)
- After the children find the bag with lettuce, ask: "What problem do the children have?" (*They can't find Brownie and don't know what happened to the nest and eggs.*) Follow-up: "Turn and talk with a partner about what you think might have happened."
- After the children find information about turtles on the computer, ask: "What information do the photographs and captions give you?" (*They show you what real turtles look like and give more information about each turtle.*)
- At the end of the story, ask: "What did you learn from this story? Turn and talk with a partner about your thinking."

MINILESSON Conclusions

TEACH Display the minilesson principle on chart paper, and read it aloud to students. Explain that authors give details in a story to help readers figure out things they don't say. Remind students that when they figure out something that the author did not say, they have drawn a conclusion.

1. Discuss the principle with students, using an example from *Mystery at Reed's Pond*. Suggested language: "The children find a paper bag with lettuce in it. The author didn't say who left the bag and why there was lettuce in it, but you can figure it out. You know that people carry things in paper bags. You also know that pet turtles eat lettuce. This information helps you know that someone might have had a turtle in the bag."

> **MINILESSON PRINCIPLE**
> Readers notice that they can use details in a story to figure out things the author does not say.

2. Guide students to draw conclusions about how Adrian felt about turtles. Help students recognize details that helped them know that Adrian likes turtles. (*He was the first to spot Brownie. He was worried when they didn't find him and happy when they saw him again.*)
3. Work with students to draw other conclusions using details from the story. Have students tell which details helped them figure out things that the author didn't say.
4. Record students' responses on an Inference Map like the one shown here.

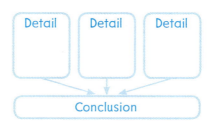

SUMMARIZE AND APPLY Restate the minilesson principle. Then tell students to apply it to their independent reading. Suggested language: "When you read, think about details in the story that can help you figure out things the author doesn't say."

GROUP SHARE Ask students to share a story from their reading. Have them tell about something they figured out that the author didn't say. Then have them name details in the story that helped them figure it out.

98 • Lesson 30

Lesson 30

▶ A Big Python Problem

INTERACTIVE READ-ALOUD/SHARED READING

Read aloud the selection to students. Stop periodically for brief discussion of the text. Use the following suggested stopping points and prompts:

- After reading the section A Dangerous Predator, ask: "What information do the photo and caption give you about pythons?" (*They show what a python looks like and tell how much they can weigh.*)
- After reading the section Can the Problem Be Solved?, ask: "Do you think the author thinks that the python problem can be solved? Turn and talk with a partner about why you think so."
- At the end of the selection, ask: "Why do you think the author wrote this selection? Turn and talk about your thinking with a partner."

MINILESSON Genre: Informational Text

TEACH Display the minilesson principle on chart paper, and read it aloud to students. Tell students that authors often share problems and ways to solve them.

1. Explain to students that authors often write about a problem because they believe it is an important problem to solve. They want readers to agree that the problem is important.

> **MINILESSON PRINCIPLE**
>
> Readers notice when an author shares a problem and how to solve it.

2. Focus on the first section of *A Big Python Problem*. Guide students to understand what the problem is. Suggested language: "The author tells about pet pythons and how people are letting them loose in the Everglades. This is the problem the author is sharing."
3. Work with students to tell the information the author shares about how to solve this problem. Guide them to understand that park officials are using radio transmitters and dogs to help them find and catch the pythons.

SUMMARIZE AND APPLY Restate the minilesson principle. Tell students to apply it to their independent reading. Suggested language: "When you read a selection, think about the problems and solutions that the author shares."

GROUP SHARE Have students tell about a problem and solution the author shared in something they read.

▶ Poetry Place

INTERACTIVE READ-ALOUD/SHARED READING

Read aloud the poems to students. Stop periodically for brief discussion of the text. Use the following suggested stopping points and prompts:

- After reading "Naming the Turtle," ask: "What does this poem tell about?" (*names to give to different kinds of turtles*) Follow-up: "How does the poet make the poem interesting?"
- After reading "Greater Flamingo," ask: "What does the poet mean by the phrase *pale as the pink lip of a shell*?" (*The author is describing the color of the flamingo by comparing it to the part of a shell near its opening.*) Follow-up: "How does the poet describe the water?" (*cool and green*)

MINILESSON Genre: Poetry

TEACH Display the minilesson principle on chart paper, and read it aloud to students. Remind students that poems can make readers feel a certain way. Tell them they will think about how a poem makes them feel.

1. Explain to students that different words can make them feel different ways. Have them name words that make them feel excited, sad, or scared. Remind students that poets choose words carefully to create different feelings in readers.

> **MINILESSON PRINCIPLE**
>
> Readers think about how a poem makes them feel.

2. Reread "Naming the Turtle." Suggested language: "This poem tells about different names for turtles. How does the poem make you feel?" Guide students to understand that the poem makes readers think about all the different characteristics of turtles.
3. Focus on "Greater Flamingo." Ask: "How does this poem make you feel? Turn and talk about your thinking with a partner." Guide students to understand that the image in the poem may give them a feeling of calm or serenity.

SUMMARIZE AND APPLY Restate the minilesson principle. Tell students to apply it to their independent reading. Suggested language: "When you read a poem, think about how the poem makes you feel."

GROUP SHARE Ask students to share a poem they read. Have them tell how the poem made them feel.

Whole-Group Lessons • **99**

Teacher's Notes

Teaching Genre

Genre instruction and repeated exposure to a variety of genres are essential components of any high-quality literacy program. Access to the tools students need to understand information in different genres will make them better readers. When students understand the characteristics of a variety of genres, they will be able to:

• gain an appreciation for a wide range of texts
• develop a common vocabulary for talking about texts
• begin reading texts with a set of expectations related to genre
• make evidence-based predictions
• develop preferences as readers
• understand purposes for reading and writing
• recognize the choices an author makes when writing
• compare and contrast texts
• think deeply about what they read

The pages in this section provide a framework for discussing genre with your students in an age-appropriate way. You can use the lists on the following pages to organize for genre discussion.

• **Genre Characteristics:** teach and review the salient features
• **Discussion Starters:** begin and maintain productive discussions
• **Comparing Texts:** encourage students to make connections across texts
• **Literature:** select *Journeys* literature for discussion

Realistic Fiction	102	Play	107
Historical Fiction	103	Informational Text	108
Traditional Tale	104	Biography	110
Fantasy	105	Poetry	111
Science Fiction	106		

Realistic Fiction

SUPPORT THINKING

DISCUSSION STARTERS During whole-group and small-group discussion, use questions to spark conversation about genre characteristics.

- Who is telling the story?
- Who are the main characters in the story?
- What is [character name] like? How can you tell?
- What problem does [character name] have?
- How does [character name]'s problem get solved by the end of the story?
- How does [character name] change from the beginning of the story to the end?
- What are the most important events in the story?
- How are the story's events like things that could happen in real life?
- How is the story's setting like a real place?
- What lesson do the characters learn? What lesson do you learn from reading the story?

COMPARING TEXTS After students have read and listened to several realistic fiction stories, prompt them to compare selections and to recognize common characteristics. Use questions such as these:

- What do the characters in [title] and [title] have in common?
- What could [character name] learn from [character name from another story]?
- How are the themes of [title] and [title] different?
- Which realistic fiction stories that you have read make you want to read more stories by the same author? What do you like most about them?

Because of Winn-Dixie, Student Book, Lesson 1

Me and Uncle Romie, Student Book, Lesson 8

Genre Characteristics

Realistic fiction is a made-up story that could really happen in today's world.

Through repeated exposure to realistic fiction, students should learn to notice common genre characteristics. Use friendly language to help them understand the following concepts:

- **Author's Purpose:** to entertain
- **Characters:** characters are like real people and may remind students of people they know; readers learn about characters through the author's descriptions and by thinking about what the characters think, say, and do
- **Setting:** where and when the story takes place; could be based on a real place
- **Plot:** events that could really happen; includes a problem or conflict that characters face, a series of events that occur as characters try to solve the problem, and a resolution
- **Dialogue:** the words that characters say reveal what they are like and what other characters are like
- **Point of View:** the narrator or speaker of the story; in first-person point of view, the narrator is part of the story; in third-person point of view, the narrator is an outside observer who tells the story
- **Theme:** the story's message, or what the author is trying to say to readers; theme can often be determined through what characters in the story learn

JOURNEYS Literature

STUDENT BOOK
Because of Winn-Dixie
Dear Mr. Winston
How Tía Lola Came to Stay
Me and Uncle Romie
Moon Runner

STUDENT MAGAZINE
The Girl Who Loved Spiders

TEACHER'S EDITION READ-ALOUD
Bookmobile Rescue
Darnell Tries Harder
Hannah in California

Jazzy Jasmine
New Friends in the Classroom
Safe from Harm
Sideline Support

LEVELED READERS
Baseball Boys **P**
Baseball Friends **P**
The Friendship Garden **S**
A Gift for Grandpa **S**
Gramp's Favorite Gift **S**
I Will Not Eat That! **R**
My Sister's Surprise **T**
The Mystery on Maple Street **Q**

New Kid on the Court **N**
Painting the Ocean **M**
Parker's Problem **P**
The Picky Eater **R**
Recipe for Learning **M**
Sisters Play Soccer **R**
Soccer Sisters **R**
Stuck at Camp **S**
Tammy's Goal **N**
Think Before You Speak **S**
Trading Talents **S**
What Happened on Maple Street? **Q**

102 • Teaching Genre: Realistic Fiction

Historical Fiction

Genre Characteristics

Historical fiction is a made-up story that could have happened in a real time and place in the past.

Through repeated exposure to historical fiction, students should learn to notice common genre characteristics. Use friendly language to help them understand the following concepts:

- **Author's Purpose:** to entertain
- **Characters:** characters are realistic, but they may look or talk like people from the past; readers learn about characters through the author's descriptions and by thinking about what the characters think, say, and do
- **Setting:** where and when the story takes place; setting is important to the story and shows something about a period or place in history
- **Plot:** what happens in the story—could contain an author's imagined details about real events; includes a problem that characters face, a series of events that occur as characters try to solve the problem, and a resolution
- **Dialogue:** the words that characters say may show how people of a certain time talked to one another—for example, formal, informal, or the use of slang
- **Point of View:** the narrator or speaker of the story; in first-person point of view, the narrator is part of the story; in third-person point of view, the narrator is an outside observer who tells the story
- **Theme:** the story's message, or what the author is trying to say to readers; theme may center around an important issue during the time in which the story takes place

Journeys Literature

STUDENT BOOK
The Earth Dragon Awakes
Riding Freedom

A Dangerous Trip **S**
Elizabeth's Stormy Ride **N**
Little Hare and the Thundering Earth **S**
A New Name for Lois **R**
Perilous Passage **S**

Sailing to Safety **N**
Two Against the Mississippi **T**

LEVELED READERS
Come to Nicodemus **S**

SUPPORT THINKING

DISCUSSION STARTERS During whole-group and small-group discussion, use questions to spark conversation about genre characteristics.

- Where and when does this story take place?
- What is important about the setting of this story?
- What is [character name] like?
- Which of [character name]'s traits help you know that he/she lived in the past?
- What happens in this story?
- What is the main problem in this story?
- How is the setting important to what happens?
- What is the author trying to tell you with this story?
- What kinds of issues were important to the people in this story?

COMPARING TEXTS After students have read and listened to several historical fiction stories, prompt them to compare selections and to recognize common characteristics. Use questions such as these:

- How are the settings in [title] and [title] different? In which time and place would you rather live?
- How are the characters in [title] and [title] different in the ways they talk, think, and act? How are they the same?
- Which historical fiction story that you've read makes you want to learn more about where and when the characters lived?

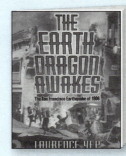 

The Earth Dragon Awakes, Student Book, Lesson 12

Riding Freedom, Student Book, Lesson 16

Traditional Tale

SUPPORT THINKING

DISCUSSION STARTERS During whole-group and small-group discussion, use questions to spark conversation about genre characteristics.

- Who are the main characters in this story? Who are the minor characters?
- Which characters have qualities that represent good? How can you tell?
- How do the characters in the story change from the beginning to the end?
- What lesson does the author want you to learn by reading this story? How could you apply the lesson to your life?
- What does this story help you learn about the people or group that first told the story long ago?

COMPARING TEXTS After students have read and listened to several traditional tales, prompt them to compare selections and to recognize common characteristics. Use questions such as these:

- Which characters in [title] and [title] have something in common?
- Why do you think the lessons in stories like [title] and [title] have been shared for many years?
- Think about the ending of [title]. How is this ending similar to the ending of [title]? How is it different?

Stormalong, Student Book, Lesson 5

The Dove and the Ant, Student Book, Lesson 14

Genre Characteristics

Traditional tales are short, made-up stories that have been retold over and over for many years.

Through repeated exposure to traditional tales, students should learn to notice common genre characteristics. Use friendly language to help them understand the following concepts:

- **Author's Purpose:** to entertain; to teach a lesson
- **Characters:** characters could be like real people or they could have exaggerated traits or amazing abilities; talking animals and objects are common in traditional tales; characters are usually good or evil
- **Setting:** usually set long ago in a specific place (often where the story originated)
- **Plot:** what happens in the story; could have magical elements or events that are unrealistic; includes a problem that characters face, a series of events that occur as characters try to solve the problem, and a resolution
- **Theme:** the lesson that the author wants to teach readers; often tells about the beliefs of a group of people; may explain how something came to be
- **Variants:** different versions of the same story may be told in different cultures and places
- **Subgenres:** can be classified into subgenres such as fable, folktale, fairy tale, tall tale, trickster tale, myth—each having its own unique features

Journeys Literature

STUDENT BOOK
The Dove and the Ant
Hoderi the Fisherman
Once Upon a Cool Motorcycle Dude
The Sticky Coyote
Stormalong

STUDENT MAGAZINE
The Frog and the Milk Pail

TEACHER'S EDITION READ-ALOUD
Mighty Joe Magarac

LEVELED READERS
The Amazing Balina **P**
Balina **Q**
The Lark Sings in Many Colors **T**
Mississippi Marvis Barnes **P**

A Pen and a Painting **S**
Rosa's Adventure **S**
Whisper **R**

104 • Teaching Genre: Traditional Tale

Fantasy

Genre Characteristics

A fantasy is a made-up story that could not happen in real life.

Through repeated exposure to fantasy, students should learn to notice common genre characteristics. Use friendly language to help them understand the following concepts:

- **Author's Purpose:** to entertain
- **Characters:** characters often have human qualities but can do amazing or magical things; animals and objects may have human characteristics and may talk; the main character usually has a goal to accomplish
- **Setting:** often set in a different time, in a magical or imaginary world, or both
- **Plot:** what happens in the story could not happen in the real world, but the plot is believable in the world that the author has created; includes a problem, a series of events that occur as characters try to solve the problem, and a resolution; the problem may be a fight against evil characters who get in the way of a goal
- **Theme:** the lesson that the author wants to teach readers

Journeys Literature

STUDENT BOOK
The World According to Humphrey

TEACHER'S EDITION READ-ALOUD
Tim Wishes Twice

LEVELED READERS
The Beltons' Imagination **Q**
A Dragon's View **S**
The Magic of Teamwork **M**
The Princess and the Manatee **O**
The Seal Who Wanted to Live **O**
Summer with Uncle Vince **Q**

SUPPORT THINKING

DISCUSSION STARTERS During whole-group and small-group discussion, use questions to spark conversation about genre characteristics.

- What is special about the setting of this story?
- Which events in this story could not really happen? How do you know?
- Which characters in this story could not be a part of a realistic fiction story? Explain.
- What is [character name] trying to do in this story? Who or what is getting in the way?
- Why is the setting of the story important to what happens?
- How is [character name]'s problem resolved by the end of the story?

COMPARING TEXTS After students have read and listened to several fantasy stories, prompt them to compare selections and to recognize common characteristics. Use questions such as these:

- Would you rather be a character in the story [title] or [title]? Explain.
- How are [fantasy title] and [realistic fiction title] alike? How are they different?
- Are the characters in [title] or [title] closer to being like people in the real world? Explain your thinking.

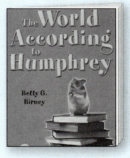

The World According to Humphrey, Student Book, Lesson 21

Teaching Genre: Fantasy • **105**

Science Fiction

SUPPORT THINKING

DISCUSSION STARTERS During whole-group and small-group discussion, use questions to spark conversation about genre characteristics.

- Where does the story take place?
- When does the story take place?
- How is the world the author has created different from today's world?
- What words and images does the author use to help you imagine the setting?
- What problem does the setting create for the characters?
- What part does science or technology have in helping the characters solve the problem?
- What do you learn about the characters by what they say and do?
- What is the author trying to tell you with this story?
- Which events in this story could happen in today's world? Which events could not happen in today's world?

COMPARING TEXTS After students have read and listened to several science fiction stories, prompt them to compare selections and to recognize common characteristics. Use questions such as these:

- How are the worlds created by the authors in [title] and [title] different?
- How are the problems in [title] and [title] different?
- How are the messages in [title] and [title] different? Why do you think the authors used a time in the future to teach these lessons?

The Fun They Had, Student Book, Lesson 25

Genre Characteristics

Science fiction is a made-up story that is based on scientific ideas or technology.

Through repeated exposure to science fiction, students should learn to notice common genre characteristics. Use friendly language to help them understand the following concepts:

- **Author's Purpose:** to entertain
- **Characters:** characters may be people, animals, or objects that have human problems but can do or experience things that are not realistic in today's world
- **Setting:** description of setting shows the author's ideas about what it would be like to live in the future or on another planet
- **Plot:** events are usually driven by what happens to characters as a result of the author's imagined world; includes a problem that characters face, a series of events that occur as characters try to solve the problem, and a resolution
- **Theme:** what the author is trying to say to readers

Journeys Literature

STUDENT BOOK
The Fun They Had

LEVELED READERS
Dex Is a Hero **S**

A Hero Weighs In **S**
The Linney Twins Get Cooking **M**
Math Today and Tomorrow **T**

106 • Teaching Genre: Science Fiction

Play

Genre Characteristics

A play is a story that is meant to be performed for an audience.

Through repeated exposure to plays, students should learn to notice common genre characteristics. Use friendly language to help them understand the following concepts:

- **Author's Purpose:** to entertain
- **Characters:** portrayed by the actors in the play; may include a narrator who provides background information and fills in details about the characters, setting, or events
- **Stage Directions:** notes from the writer of the play that tell actors how to move or with what emotion certain lines should be read; give information about how to set up the stage for the play, including props to use and what the actors might wear; stage directions usually appear in parentheses and in italic type
- **Dialogue:** the conversations between characters that are read aloud by actors; a play is made up almost entirely of dialogue
- **Plot:** the action of the story, or what happens, as revealed through dialogue and stage directions; may be based on real events and people or made up by the writer
- **Setting:** can be any place, real or imaginary; usually described in stage directions
- **Acts:** large sections of a play between breaks; can be further divided into scenes
- **Scene:** a part of the play in which the setting does not change

Journeys Literature

STUDENT BOOK
Hoderi the Fisherman
In the Wild
The Power of W.O.W.!
Save Timber Woods!
Sidewalk Artists
Working for the Vote

LEVELED READERS
A.L.L. to the Rescue **S**
A Friendly Field Trip **P**
Friends on a Field Trip **O**
Nina Wows KWOW **N**

SUPPORT THINKING

DISCUSSION STARTERS During whole-group and small-group discussion, use questions to spark conversation about genre characteristics.

- What information does the writer give at the beginning of the play?
- What is the narrator's role in this play?
- Who are the most important characters? Why do you think so?
- What information do you learn about the characters from the stage directions?
- How do the stage directions help you understand the setting?
- What is the most exciting part of the play? Explain.
- If you were to act in this play, which character would you want to play? How would you use the stage directions to help you with your role?

COMPARING TEXTS After students have read and listened to several plays, prompt them to compare selections and to recognize common characteristics. Use questions such as these:

- How do the writers of [title] and [title] help you understand what is happening in the play?
- How are the settings of [title] and [title] different?
- In which play—[title] or [title]—do you think the dialogue is more realistic? Explain.
- What would it be like to have [character] and [character from another play] in the same play?

 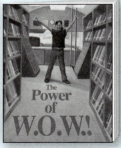

Hoderi the Fisherman, Student Book, Lesson 5

The Power of W.O.W.! Student Book, Lesson 18

Teaching Genre: Play • **107**

Informational Text

Genre Characteristics

Informational text gives facts about real people, places, things, or events.

Through repeated exposure to informational texts, students should learn to notice common genre characteristics. Use friendly language to help them understand the following concepts:

- **Author's Purpose:** to inform; to persuade
- **Illustrations/Photographs:** show the information being described accurately and help readers understand the ideas in the text
- **Graphic Features:** images that help the reader understand information in the text or show additional information; may include the following:
  - **Diagrams:** pictures with labels that identify or explain specific parts
  - **Maps:** pictures that are used to show the physical layout of an area
  - **Charts/Graphs:** information arranged in a way that helps readers compare pieces of information or data
  - **Timeline:** shows the important events related to a topic over a period of time
- **Text Features:** special text that helps the reader understand what is important; may include the following:
  - **Headings:** type—usually larger, darker, or both—at the beginning of a new section; used to organize information into sections that make sense for the topic
  - **Captions:** words or sentences that explain an image
  - **Special Type:** the author may emphasize words and ideas by using a different color or size or by using bold or italic print
- **Main Idea:** what the text is mostly about
- **Details:** smaller ideas that support the main idea and tell more about the topic
- **Text Structure:** the text's overall structure
  - **Narrative:** can be organized and have the feeling of a story with a clear beginning, middle, and end
  - **Sequence:** events or steps in a process are told in order
  - **Compare/Contrast:** the author's main goal is to tell how things are alike and different
  - **Cause/Effect:** the author explains a topic by telling about something that happened and why it happened
  - **Problem/Solution:** the author explains a problem and offers a solution to the problem; details support the author's solution
  - **Description:** the author explains what something is and what it is like
- **Facts:** pieces of information that are true and can be proved
- **Opinions:** statements of how the author feels about a subject; may be used to try to persuade readers

SUPPORT THINKING

DISCUSSION STARTERS During whole-group and small-group discussion, use questions to spark conversation about genre characteristics.

- What different kinds of graphic features does the author use to help you understand the topic?
- How does the author use size and colors of type to show what is important?
- What is the selection mostly about?
- How is the selection organized? How can you tell?
- How does the author make the information in this selection interesting?
- Which of the author's ideas are opinions? How does the author support his/her opinions?
- How does the author feel about the topic? How do you know?
- What kind of research do you think the author did to write this selection?

COMPARING TEXTS After students have read and listened to several informational texts, prompt them to compare selections and to recognize common characteristics. Use questions such as these:

- How do the authors of [title] and [title] use text and graphic features in different ways?
- Which selection—[title] or [title]—makes you want to find out more about the topic? Explain.
- How do the authors of [title] and [title] organize the text in different ways? How does the organization help you understand the ideas?
- How can you tell that [author] and [author] think their topics are important?

Coming Distractions: Questioning Movies, Student Book, Lesson 7

The Life and Times of the Ant, Student Book, Lesson 14

JOURNEYS Literature

STUDENT BOOK

Antarctic Journal: Four Months at the Bottom of the World

Because of BookEnds

Coming Distractions: Questioning Movies

The Coolest Marathon

A Day for the Moon

Ecology for Kids

The Edible Schoolyard

The Ever-Living Tree

Field Guide to Snakes of the Southwest

Knowing Noses: Search-and-Rescue Dogs

The Life and Times of the Ant

Make the Switch

Owen and Mzee

Pizza Pizzazz

The Right Dog for the Job

The Screech Owl Who Liked Television

Sea Sanctuary

Spindletop

Storyteller Diane Ferlatte

Technology for All Learners

The Wonder of Animation

STUDENT MAGAZINE

Amphibian Alert!

A Big Python Problem

John Muir: A Persuasive Essay

Making the Most from Trash

Museums: Worlds of Wonder

Web Wise

TEACHER'S EDITION READ-ALOUD

Deserts on the Move?

Forests Are Forever

Frisky Whiskers

Fun and Games on the Range

The Future of Flight

Is Sasquatch Out There?

On My Way to Meet the Khan:

Excerpts from Marco Polo's Adventures

Race Against Death

Steven Spielberg: A Filmmaker's Journey

Texas Twisters

Wicked Wind

LEVELED READERS

All About Hamsters R

Amazing Birds of Antarctica O

Andrew Carnegie U

Animal Doctors N

Animals Helping People N

Animals of the Redwood Forest S

Antarctica, Land of Possibility U

Ants, Aphids, and Caterpillars S

Ants of All Kinds O

Arthropods Everywhere! S

Arthropods Rule! S

Artists in Training P

Behind the Scenes P

Birds of Prey in North America U

Champions on Ice S

Check Out the Library N

Community Teamwork O

Critics in Hollywood V

Dangerous Waves P

The Daring Riders of the Pony Express U

Earthquake Scientists T

Entertainment Then and Now U

Feathered Hunters of the Night Q

The First Lady of Track O

Firsts in Forecasting T

Flamenco, Olé! U

Flying into History P

Forever Green P

Gale and Brian, Friends Forever S

Gentle Redwood Giants S

Going Wild at the Zoo R

The Golden Age of Sail P

A Great Partnership T

Helen Keller's Lifelong Friend S

Helen Keller's Special Friend S

Helping Wild Animals T

Heroes of the Antarctic V

Hooray for Hollywood U

How Smart Are Animals? U

How Women Got the Vote U

An Icy Adventure R

An Inside Look at Zoos S

Inside the Zoo R

Isaac Asimov W

Keeping Safe in an Earthquake O

Koko Communicates O

Lewis and Clark's Packing List Q

Life Among the Redwoods S

The Lives of Social Insects P

Love Those Bugs! T

The Magic of Movies T

Making Movies T

Mill Girls S

Now Showing in Your Living Room P

Peaceful Protest U

Plants of the Redwood Forest O

Protecting Endangered Animals T

Really, Really Cold! O

Remarkable Robots P

Reptiles As Pets O

Romare Bearden R

A Rural Veterinarian R

Separate Worlds Q

Squash in the Schoolyard N

Stagecoach Travel Q

Storytelling Through the Years Q

Taking Care of Animals R

A Taste of the Dominican Republic S

A Time to Unite V

Tough Times S

Tracing the Harlem Renaissance W

The Truth About Rodents R

A Visit to Antarctica R

A Visit to the Dominican Republic N

When Tsunamis Strike T

The Wonderful World of Camouflage U

Why We Need Trees T

You're On Camera T

Teaching Genre: Informational Text • **109**

Biography

SUPPORT THINKING

DISCUSSION STARTERS During whole-group and small-group discussion, use questions to spark conversation about genre characteristics.

- Who is this biography about?
- What is the subject like?
- What are [subject name]'s strengths? What are [subject name]'s weaknesses?
- Where did [subject name] live?
- How did other people influence [subject name] and affect his/her life?
- What did other people think about [subject name]?
- What can you tell about [subject name] by what he/she says?
- Why is it important to know about [subject name]'s life?
- What does the author think about [subject]?

COMPARING TEXTS After students have read and listened to several biographies, prompt them to compare selections and to recognize common characteristics. Use questions such as these:

- What things about [subject name] and [subject name] are alike? What things are different?
- If you were to meet [subject name], what questions would you ask him/her? How would the questions be different from questions you might ask [different subject name]?
- Which author do you think had more difficult research to do about the subject? Why do you think so?

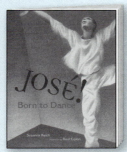

José! Born to Dance, Student Book, Lesson 10

Sacagawea, Student Book, Lesson 20

Genre Characteristics

A biography is the true story of a real person's life.

Through repeated exposure to biographies, students should learn to notice common genre characteristics. Use friendly language to help them understand the following concepts:

- **Author's Purpose:** to inform; to show why this person's life is important
- **Characters:** the real person the biography is about is the subject; a biography tells what the subject accomplished and why he or she is important; other characters in the biography are real people who influenced the life of the subject in some way
- **Setting:** thinking about the time and place in which the subject lived will help readers understand more about the person
- **Narrative Structure:** events are told in order as a story; events may span the person's entire life or may represent a specific time in the person's life
- **Facts and Opinions:** most parts of a biography are facts that are accurate and can be proved; the author's opinions may be included
- **Point of View:** usually third-person point of view—the narrator is an outside observer who tells the story

JOURNEYS Literature

STUDENT BOOK

Harvesting Hope: The Story of Cesar Chavez
I Could Do That! Esther Morris Gets Women the Vote
José! Born to Dance
My Brother Martin: A Sister Remembers Growing Up with the Rev. Dr. Martin Luther King Jr.
Sacagawea

TEACHER'S EDITION READ-ALOUD

The Father of India
Getting the Story

Jane's Big Ideas
Let Me Be Brave
Mexican Dove
The Troublemaker Who Healed a Nation

LEVELED READERS

A Champion of Change **S**
Chief Washakie **U**
The First Woman Doctor **P**
Isadora Duncan **O**
Jackson Pollock in Action **S**
John Wesley Powell **O**
Laura Ingalls Wilder **R**
A Leader for All **U**
The Life of Jackson Pollock **S**
Luciano Pavarotti **W**
The People's President **R**
A President for the People **R**
Sharing a Dream **O**
Shirley Chisholm **S**
Songs for the People **P**
The Story of Dorothea Lange **U**
Thurgood Marshall **S**
A Voice for Equality **S**
Writer from the Prairie **R**
The Writer Who Changed America **U**

Poetry

Genre Characteristics

Poetry is a piece of writing in which words and their sounds are used to show images and express feelings and ideas.

Through repeated exposure to poetry, students should learn to notice common genre characteristics. Use friendly language to help them understand the following concepts:

- **Author's Purpose:** to entertain or express
- **Form:** includes free verse, narrative, lyric, haiku
- **Stanzas:** the sections of a poem; a stanza may focus on one central idea or thought; lines in a stanza are arranged in a way that looks and sounds pleasing
- **Rhyme:** words that have the same ending sound may be used at the ends of lines to add interest to the poem and to make it fun to read
- **Rhythm:** the beat of how the words are read; may be fast or slow
- **Sensory Words:** words that describe how things look, feel, taste, smell, and sound
- **Figurative Language:** similes, metaphors, and personification; the comparison of things that might not ordinarily seem similar
- **Onomatopoeia:** the use of words that imitate the sounds they describe
- **Alliteration:** the repetition of the same initial consonant sounds
- **Punctuation:** tells a reader when to pause; can make a poem sound short and choppy or long and flowing; may not be present at all

JOURNEYS Literature

STUDENT BOOK
Dance to the Beat
Langston Hughes: A Poet and a Dreamer
Native American Nature Poetry
Towering Trees

STUDENT MAGAZINE
The Comb of Trees
Dinosaur Bone
Enjoy the Earth
Greater Flamingo
Museum Farewell
Naming the Turtle
The Poison-Dart Frogs
The Spider
Spider Ropes
Toad by the Road

SUPPORT THINKING

DISCUSSION STARTERS During whole-group and small-group discussion, use questions to spark conversation about genre characteristics.

- What does this poem describe?
- Which words in the poem help you picture or experience what the poet describes?
- Which words in the poem describe sounds? Which words describe smells? Which words describe tastes?
- How does the poem make you feel?
- How would you describe the rhythm of the poem? What feeling does the rhythm give you when you read the poem?
- Which of the poem's images do you like best? Why?
- How does the title of the poem fit what the poem says?
- What kinds of decisions did the writer of this poem make as he/she wrote it?

COMPARING TEXTS After students have read and listened to several poems, prompt them to compare poems and to recognize common characteristics. Use questions such as these:

- How are the images in [title] and [title] different?
- How do the writers of [title] and [title] create poems with different feelings?
- How are the shapes or forms of [title] and [title] different?

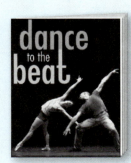 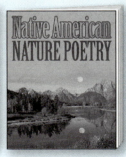

Dance to the Beat, Student Book, Lesson 10

Native American Nature Poetry, Student Book, Lesson 20

Leveled Readers Database

Guided Reading Level	Title	Grade Pack	DRA Level	Lexile Level	Genre	Word Count
M	Ike in the Spotlight	4 ●	28	590	Fairy Tale	992
M	Linney Twins Get Cooking, The	4 ●	28	610	Science Fiction	968
M	Magic of Teamwork, The	4 ●	28	530	Fantasy	873
M	Painting the Ocean	4 ●	28	400	Realistic Fiction	885
M	Recipe for Learning	4 ●	28	620	Realistic Fiction	879
N	Animal Doctors	4 ●	30	710	Narrative Nonfiction	801
N	Animals Helping People	4VR	34	940	Informational Text	1,016
N	Check Out the Library	4VR	30	820	Informational Text	839
N	Elizabeth's Stormy Ride	4 ●	34	310	Historical Fiction	815
N	New Kid on the Court	4 ●	30	460	Realistic Fiction	776
N	Nina Wows KWOW	4 ●	30	NP	Play	791
N	Sailing to Safety	4 ●	34	560	Historical Fiction	1,005
N	Squash in the Schoolyard	4VR	34	700	Informational Text	620
N	Tammy's Goal	4 ●	30	500	Realistic Fiction	921
N	Visit to the Dominican Republic, A	4VR	34	630	Informational Text	601
O	Amazing Birds of Antarctica	4 ●	38	650	Narrative Nonfiction	759
O	Ants of All Kinds	4VR	38	890	Informational Text	898
O	Community Teamwork	4VR	38	910	Informational Text	1,101
O	First Lady of Track, The	4VR	38	760	Informational Text	885
O	Friends on a Field Trip	4 ◆	38	NP	Play	1,266
O	Isadora Duncan	4 ●	38	780	Biography	915
O	John Wesley Powell	4 ●	38	830	Biography	888
O	Keeping Safe in an Earthquake	4VR	38	780	Informational Text	949
O	Koko Communicates	4 ●	38	800	Narrative Nonfiction	822
O	Plants of the Redwood Forest	4 ●	38	730	Informational Text	913
O	Princess and the Manatee, The	4 ■	38	710	Fantasy	1,655
O	Really, Really Cold!	4VR	38	690	Informational Text	781
O	Reptiles As Pets	4VR	38	800	Informational Text	1,109
O	Seal Who Wanted to Live, The	4 ●	38	520	Fantasy	846
O	Sharing a Dream	4 ●	38	830	Biography	913

ONLINE LEVELED READERS DATABASE

- Go to www.thinkcentral.com for the complete *Journeys* Online Leveled Readers Database.
- Search by grade, genre, title, or level.

Author's Purpose	Cause and Effect	Compare and Contrast	Conclusions	Fact and Opinion	Main Ideas and Details	Sequence of Events	Story Structure	Text and Graphic Features	Theme	Understanding Characters
		●	●			●	●		●	●
●	●	●	●			●	●			●
●	●	●	●			●	●		●	
	●	●	●			●	●		●	●
●			●			●	●		●	●
●		●	●	●	●		●	●		
●	●	●	●		●	●				
●				●	●					
●	●		●			●	●		●	●
●	●	●	●			●	●		●	●
●	●	●	●			●	●		●	●
●	●	●	●			●	●		●	●
●	●	●		●			●			
●	●		●			●	●		●	●
●		●	●		●	●		●		
●	●	●	●	●	●	●		●		
●		●	●	●	●	●				
●	●					●				
●	●		●			●	●			
●		●	●			●	●		●	●
●	●	●	●	●	●	●		●		
●	●	●	●		●	●		●		
●	●					●		●		
●	●		●	●	●	●		●		
●	●		●	●		●		●		
●	●		●			●	●		●	●
●	●	●				●		●		
●	●		●		●	●		●		
	●		●			●	●		●	●
●	●		●		●	●		●		

Leveled Readers Database • **113**

Leveled Readers Database

Guided Reading Level	Title	Grade Pack	DRA Level	Lexile Level	Genre	Word Count
P	Amazing Balina, The	4 ◆	38	660	Tall Tale	1,379
P	Artists in Training	4VR	38	790	Informational Text	813
P	Baseball Boys	4 ▲	38	680	Realistic Fiction	1,146
P	Baseball Friends	4 ◆	38	610	Realistic Fiction	1,211
P	Behind the Scenes	4VR	38	930	Informational Text	894
P	Dangerous Waves	4VR	38	670	Informational Text	915
P	Father's Garden, A	4 ◆	38	600	Fiction	1,129
P	First Woman Doctor, The	4 ●	38	650	Biography	880
P	Flying into History	4 ●	38	790	Narrative Nonfiction	846
P	Forever Green	4VR	38	930	Informational Text	846
P	Friendly Field Trip, A	4 ▲	38	NP	Play	1,278
P	Golden Age of Sail, The	4VR	38	720	Informational Text	870
P	Lives of Social Insects, The	4 ●	38	910	Informational Text	886
P	Mississippi Marvis Barnes	4 ●	38	360	Tall Tale	874
P	Now Showing in Your Living Room	4 ●	38	800	Informational Text	885
P	Parker's Problem	4 ●	38	430	Realistic Fiction	850
P	Remarkable Robots	4VR	38	950	Informational Text	994
P	Songs for the People	4 ●	38	810	Biography	871
Q	Balina	4 ▲	40	600	Tall Tale	1,325
Q	Beltons' Imagination, The	4 ▲	40	780	Fantasy	1,506
Q	Dad's Garden	4 ▲	40	630	Fiction	1,104
Q	Feathered Hunters of the Night	4VR	40	1050	Informational Text	959
Q	Lewis and Clark's Packing List	4VR	40	810	Informational Text	936
Q	Mystery on Maple Street, The	4 ▲	40	490	Realistic Fiction	1,153
Q	Separate Worlds	4VR	40	730	Informational Text	858
Q	Stagecoach Travel	4VR	40	680	Informational Text	916
Q	Storytelling Through the Years	4VR	40	850	Informational Text	930
Q	Summer with Uncle Vince	4 ◆	40	610	Fantasy	1,497
Q	What Happened on Maple Street?	4 ◆	40	370	Realistic Fiction	1,252
R	All About Hamsters	4CY	40	1020	Informational Text	1,710

114 • Leveled Readers Database

ONLINE LEVELED READERS DATABASE

- Go to www.thinkcentral.com for the complete *Journeys* Online Leveled Readers Database.
- Search by grade, genre, title, or level.

Author's Purpose	Cause and Effect	Compare and Contrast	Conclusions	Fact and Opinion	Main Ideas and Details	Sequence of Events	Story Structure	Text and Graphic Features	Theme	Understanding Characters
●			●			●	●		●	●
●		●	●		●					
	●						●		●	●
	●						●		●	●
●	●		●		●			●		
●	●		●		●	●				
●	●		●				●		●	●
●	●	●	●	●	●	●		●		
●	●		●		●	●		●		
●			●	●			●	●	●	●
●	●	●				●				
●	●		●		●			●		
●			●			●	●		●	●
●	●	●	●	●	●	●	●	●		
			●		●		●	●		●
●			●		●			●		
●	●		●	●	●	●		●		
●			●				●	●		●
●	●	●	●			●	●		●	●
●	●		●				●		●	●
●			●		●			●		
●			●	●	●			●		
	●		●			●	●		●	●
	●		●		●			●		
●					●					
●			●		●	●				
●	●		●			●	●		●	
	●		●			●	●		●	●
	●		●		●					

Leveled Readers Database

Guided Reading Level	Title	Grade Pack	DRA Level	Lexile Level	Genre	Word Count
R	Going Wild at the Zoo	4 ▲	40	930	Narrative Nonfiction	1,320
R	I Will Not Eat That!	4 ◆	40	380	Realistic Fiction	1,344
R	Icy Adventure, An	4 ▲	40	980	Narrative Nonfiction	1,176
R	Inside the Zoo	4 ◆	40	790	Narrative Nonfiction	1,322
R	Laura Ingalls Wilder	4 ◆	40	640	Biography	1,478
R	New Name for Lois, A	4 ◆	40	480	Historical Fiction	1,383
R	People's President, The	4 ▲	40	790	Biography	1,372
R	Picky Eater, The	4 ▲	40	570	Realistic Fiction	1,238
R	President for the People, A	4 ◆	40	610	Biography	1,318
R	Romare Bearden	4VR	40	890	Informational Text	1,005
R	Rural Veterinarian, A	4 ▲	40	890	Narrative Nonfiction	1,390
R	Sisters Play Soccer	4 ◆	40	430	Realistic Fiction	1,426
R	Soccer Sisters	4 ▲	40	580	Realistic Fiction	1,541
R	Taking Care of Animals	4 ◆	40	690	Narrative Nonfiction	1,343
R	Truth About Rodents, The	4VR	40	940	Informational Text	912
R	Visit to Antarctica, A	4 ◆	40	770	Narrative Nonfiction	1,162
R	Whisper	4 ■	40	620	Tall Tale	1,866
R	Writer from the Prairie	4 ▲	40	830	Biography	1,434
S	A.L.L. to the Rescue	4 ■	40	NP	Play	1,452
S	Animals of the Redwood Forest	4 ◆	40	710	Informational Text	1,484
S	Ants, Aphids, and Caterpillars	4CY	40	1010	Informational Text	1,819
S	Arthropods Everywhere!	4 ◆	40	730	Informational Text	1,304
S	Arthropods Rule!	4 ▲	40	860	Informational Text	1,337
S	Champion of Change, A	4 ▲	40	1010	Biography	1,341
S	Champions on Ice	4 ■	40	840	Narrative Nonfiction	1,880
S	Come to Nicodemus	4 ■	40	940	Historical Fiction	1,866
S	Dangerous Trip, A	4 ◆	40	640	Historical Fiction	1,359
S	Dex Is a Hero	4 ◆	40	610	Science Fiction	1,492
S	Dragon's View, A	4 ■	40	670	Fantasy	2,317
S	Friendship Garden, The	4 ■	40	720	Realistic Fiction	2,232

ONLINE LEVELED READERS DATABASE

- Go to www.thinkcentral.com for the complete *Journeys* Online Leveled Readers Database.
- Search by grade, genre, title, or level.

Author's Purpose	Cause and Effect	Compare and Contrast	Conclusions	Fact and Opinion	Main Ideas and Details	Sequence of Events	Story Structure	Text and Graphic Features	Theme	Understanding Characters
●	●		●	●	●	●		●		
●	●		●			●	●		●	●
●			●	●	●			●		
●	●		●	●	●	●		●		
●	●	●	●	●	●	●		●		
●	●	●	●			●	●		●	●
●	●		●	●	●	●		●		
●	●		●			●	●		●	●
●	●		●	●	●	●		●		
●	●		●	●	●	●		●		
●		●	●	●	●	●		●		
●		●	●			●	●			
	●	●	●			●	●		●	●
	●		●			●	●		●	●
●		●	●		●	●		●		
●	●		●		●	●	●			
●			●	●	●	●		●		
●	●	●	●	●		●	●		●	●
●	●	●	●	●	●	●		●		
●	●		●			●	●		●	●
●			●	●	●	●		●		
●	●		●			●		●		
●	●		●					●		
●	●		●			●		●		
●	●	●	●	●	●	●		●		
●	●	●	●	●	●			●		
	●		●			●	●		●	●
●	●		●			●	●		●	●
●	●	●	●			●	●			●
●	●	●	●			●	●		●	●
						●	●			●

Leveled Readers Database • 117

Leveled Readers Database

Guided Reading Level	Title	Grade Pack	DRA Level	Lexile Level	Genre	Word Count
S	Gale and Brian, Friends Forever	4CY	40	1050	Informational Text	1,984
S	Gentle Redwood Giants	4 ■	40	1160	Informational Text	1,776
S	Gift for Grandpa, A	4 ◆	40	500	Realistic Fiction	1,440
S	Gramp's Favorite Gift	4 ▲	40	810	Realistic Fiction	1,481
S	Helen Keller's Lifelong Friend	4 ▲	40	810	Narrative Nonfiction	1,377
S	Helen Keller's Special Friend	4 ◆	40	560	Narrative Nonfiction	1,472
S	Hero Weighs In, A	4 ▲	40	880	Science Fiction	1,488
S	Inside Look at Zoos, An	4 ■	40	960	Narrative Nonfiction	1,864
S	Jackson Pollock in Action	4 ▲	40	1000	Biography	1,263
S	Life Among the Redwoods	4 ▲	40	970	Informational Text	1,410
S	Life of Jackson Pollock, The	4 ◆	40	770	Biography	1,155
S	Little Hare and the Thundering Earth	4 ▲	40	850	Historical Fiction	1,426
S	Mill Girls	4VR	40	910	Informational Text	884
S	Pen and a Painting, A	4 ▲	40	650	Fairy Tale	1,444
S	Perilous Passage	4 ▲	40	800	Historical Fiction	1,273
S	Rosa's Adventure	4 ◆	40	420	Fairy Tale	1,403
S	Shirley Chisholm	4 ◆	40	730	Biography	1,396
S	Stuck at Camp	4 ■	40	840	Realistic Fiction	2,198
S	Taste of the Dominican Republic, A	4CY	40	870	Informational Text	675
S	Think Before You Speak	4 ■	40	580	Realistic Fiction	1,910
S	Thurgood Marshall	4 ◆	40	630	Biography	1,264
S	Tough Times	4VR	40	830	Informational Text	971
S	Trading Talents	4 ■	40	650	Realistic Fiction	1,952
S	Voice for Equality, A	4 ▲	40	890	Biography	1,263
T	Earthquake Scientists	4CY	44	1020	Informational Text	1,579
T	Firsts in Forecasting	4CY	44	930	Informational Text	1,439
T	Great Partnership, A	4CY	44	850	Informational Text	2,132
T	Helping Wild Animals	4 ■	44	1030	Narrative Nonfiction	2,126
T	Lark Sings in Many Colors, The	4 ■	44	910	Fairy Tale	2,159
T	Love Those Bugs!	4 ■	44	970	Informational Text	1,798

ONLINE LEVELED READERS DATABASE

- Go to www.thinkcentral.com for the complete *Journeys* Online Leveled Readers Database.
- Search by grade, genre, title, or level.

Author's Purpose	Cause and Effect	Compare and Contrast	Conclusions	Fact and Opinion	Main Ideas and Details	Sequence of Events	Story Structure	Text and Graphic Features	Theme	Understanding Characters
●	●	●	●	●	●	●				
●		●	●	●	●			●		
●	●		●			●	●		●	●
●	●		●			●	●		●	●
●	●	●	●	●	●	●		●		
●	●	●	●	●	●	●		●		
●	●	●	●			●	●	●		●
●	●	●	●	●	●	●		●		
●	●	●	●	●	●	●		●		
●	●		●	●	●	●		●		
●	●	●	●	●	●	●		●		
●	●	●	●			●	●	●	●	●
●				●		●				
	●	●	●			●	●		●	●
●	●		●			●	●		●	●
	●	●	●			●	●		●	●
●	●	●	●		●			●		
●	●	●	●			●	●		●	
●			●	●	●	●		●		
	●	●	●			●	●		●	●
	●	●	●	●	●	●	●		●	
●	●	●	●	●	●	●				
		●	●			●	●		●	●
●	●	●	●			●	●		●	
●	●			●			●			
●		●	●		●			●		
●	●		●			●				
●		●	●	●	●	●		●		
	●	●	●			●	●		●	●
●	●	●	●				●			

Leveled Readers Database • **119**

Leveled Readers Database

Guided Reading Level	Title	Grade Pack	DRA Level	Lexile Level	Genre	Word Count
T	Magic of Movies, The	4 ▲	44	800	Informational Text	1,304
T	Making Movies	4 ◆	44	590	Informational Text	1,297
T	Math Today and Tomorrow	4 ■	44	770	Science Fiction	2,035
T	My Sister's Surprise	4 ■	44	890	Realistic Fiction	2,298
T	Protecting Endangered Aminals	4CY	44	1000	Informational Text	1,928
T	Two Against the Mississippi	4 ■	44	900	Historical Fiction	2,187
T	When Tsunamis Strike	4CY	44	1020	Informational Text	1,836
T	Why We Need Trees	4CY	44	870	Informational Text	2,072
T	You're On Camera	4CY	44	830	Informational Text	1,759
U	Andrew Carnegie	4CY	44	920	Informational Text	1,621
U	Antarctica, Land of Possibility	4CY	44	1130	Informational Text	2,026
U	Birds of Prey in North America	4CY	44	1030	Informational Text	2,249
U	Chief Washakie	4 ■	44	1090	Biography	2,073
U	Daring Riders of the Pony Express, The	4CY	44	1080	Informational Text	1,853
U	Entertainment Then and Now	4CY	44	980	Informational Text	1,627
U	Flamenco, Olé!	4CY	44	970	Informational Text	1,729
U	Hooray for Hollywood	4CY	44	1030	Informational Text	1,725
U	How Smart Are Animals?	4CY	44	950	Informational Text	2,123
U	How Women Got the Vote	4CY	44	980	Informational Text	1,760
U	Leader for All, A	4 ■	44	880	Biography	1,500
U	Peaceful Protest	4CY	44	870	Informational Text	1,710
U	Story of Dorothea Lange, The	4 ■	44	880	Biography	1,954
U	Wonderful World of Camouflage, The	4CY	44	1090	Informational Text	1,792
U	Writer Who Changed America, The	4 ■	44	1000	Biography	1,976
V	Critics in Hollywood	4 ■	50	1080	Informational Text	1,800
V	Heroes of the Antarctic	4 ■	50	900	Narrative Nonfiction	1,994
V	Time to Unite, A	4CY	50	970	Informational Text	1,327
W	Isaac Asimov	4CY	60	1050	Informational Text	1,575
W	Luciano Pavarotti	4 ■	60	980	Biography	1,704
W	Tracing the Harlem Renaissance	4CY	60	1030	Informational Text	1,965

ONLINE LEVELED READERS DATABASE

- Go to www.thinkcentral.com for the complete *Journeys* Online Leveled Readers Database.
- Search by grade, genre, title, or level.

Author's Purpose	Cause and Effect	Compare and Contrast	Conclusions	Fact and Opinion	Main Ideas and Details	Sequence of Events	Story Structure	Text and Graphic Features	Theme	Understanding Characters
●	●	●	●	●	●	●		●		
●	●	●	●	●	●	●		●		
●	●	●	●			●	●			●
●	●		●			●	●		●	●
●	●		●		●			●		
●	●	●	●			●	●		●	●
●	●		●		●			●		
●		●	●	●	●					
●		●	●		●			●		
●	●	●	●	●	●	●		●		
●		●			●			●		
●		●	●		●			●		
●	●	●	●	●	●	●		●		
●			●		●	●		●		
●		●	●	●	●			●		
●			●	●	●			●		
●		●	●		●	●		●		
●	●	●	●	●	●			●		
●	●		●		●	●				
●			●		●			●		
●		●	●	●	●	●		●		
●	●		●	●	●	●		●		
●	●	●	●		●			●		
●	●	●	●	●	●	●		●		
●	●		●	●	●	●		●		
●	●	●	●	●	●	●		●		
●	●	●	●	●	●	●		●		
●	●		●	●	●	●		●		
●	●	●	●	●	●	●		●		
●	●	●	●		●	●		●		

Leveled Readers Database • **121**

Literature Discussion

For small-group literature discussion, use the suggested trade book titles on the pages that follow, or select age-appropriate texts from your library or classroom collection.

Engage students in discussions to build understanding of the text, deepen comprehension, and foster their confidence in talking about what they read. Encourage students to share their ideas about the text and also to build upon one another's ideas.

 Classic

 Science

 Social Studies

 Music

 Math

 Art

Suggested Trade Book Titles

BIOGRAPHY

Bertrand, Diane Gonzales. *Ricardo's Race/La carrera de Ricardo.* A bilingual biography of Ricardo Romo, a talented runner as a youth who later earned a Ph.D. in history and became a college president. Piñata, 2007 (32p).

Burleigh, Robert. *Paul Cézanne: A Painter's Journey.* Rejecting the opinions of others, the young Cézanne followed his own vision, becoming one of the world's greatest artists. Abrams, 2006 (31p).

Dunn, Joe. *Abraham Lincoln.* This biography of the president who saw the United States through its most divisive period is told in a graphic-novel format. Abdo & Daughters, 2007 (32p).

FitzGerald, Dawn. *Vinnie and Abraham.* Abraham Lincoln sat for Vinnie Ream, an eighteen-year-old sculptor, as she prepared to create a life-size statue that now stands in the U.S. Capitol. Charlesbridge, 2000 (48p).

Guzmán, Lila and Rick. *Ellen Ochoa: First Latina Astronaut.* In 1993, aboard the space shuttle *Discovery,* Ochoa became the first Latina astronaut. **Available in Spanish as** *Ellen Ochoa: La primera astronauta latina.* Enslow, 2006 (32p).

Guzmán, Lila and Rick. *Frida Kahlo: Painting Her Life.* This biography tells about the Mexican painter who is best known for her self-portraits. **Available in Spanish as** *Frida Kahlo: Pintó su vida.* Enslow, 2006 (32p).

Martin, Jacqueline Briggs. *Snowflake Bentley.* Wilson A. Bentley, fascinated with snow, devoted his life to photographing snowflakes. Houghton, 1998 (32p).

Miller, Barbara Kiely. *George Washington Carver.* This famous African American scientist was a dedicated professor, taught farmers how to keep their fields productive, and invented hundreds of uses for various crops. **Also available in Spanish.** Weekly Reader, 2007 (24p).

Parker, Robert Andrew. *Piano Starts Here.* This is the story of jazz virtuoso Art Tatum's enthusiasm for music as a young boy. Schwartz & Wade, 2008 (40p).

Ray, Deborah Kogan. *Down the Colorado.* John Wesley Powell became the first person to scientifically explore the Colorado River and the Grand Canyon. Farrar, 2007 (48p).

Streissguth, Tom. *Wilma Rudolph.* Stricken by polio as a child and told she would never walk again, Wilma Rudolph won multiple Olympic medals in track. Lerner, 2007 (120p).

Taylor, Gaylia. *George Crum and the Saratoga Chip.* Chef George Crum's efforts to please his customers result in the invention of the potato chip. Lee & Low, 2006 (32p).

Wyckoff, Edwin Brit. *Heart Man.* Although he worked as a janitor, Vivien Thomas was an African American medical technician who directed the first 100 open-heart surgeries. Enslow, 2008 (32p).

Yoo, Paula. *Sixteen Years in Sixteen Seconds: The Sammy Lee Story.* A Korean American boy realizes his dream to become an Olympic diving champion. Lee & Low, 2005 (32p).

Zalben, Jane Breskin. *Paths to Peace.* From Gandhi to Princess Diana and beyond, the author profiles people who have devoted their lives to helping others. Dutton, 2006 (48p).

FANTASY

Birney, Betty G. *Friendship According to Humphrey.* Humphrey, the hamster of Room 26, isn't sure what to make of the new class pet. Puffin, 2006 (150p).

Dahl, Roald. *Charlie and the Chocolate Factory.* Although there are five lucky winners of a tour through Willy Wonka's chocolate factory, Charlie is most special of all. **Available in Spanish as** *Charlie y la fábrica de chocolate.* Puffin, 2007 (176p).

Einhorn, Edward. *A Very Improbable Story.* On the morning of a big soccer match, Ethan wakes up with a cat on his head that won't move until he wins a game of probability. Charlesbridge, 2008 (32p).

Helgerson, Joseph. *Horns and Wrinkles.* Claire and her cousin Duke discover that trolls in the nearby Mississippi River are causing havoc in the community. Houghton, 2008 (240p).

Lechner, John. *Sticky Burr: Adventures in Burrwood Forest.* The adventures of Sticky and his friends are supplemented with information about forest life. Candlewick, 2008 (56p).

Selden, George. *The Cricket in Times Square.* First published in 1960, the story follows Chester Cricket as he leaves his Connecticut home and becomes "the most famous musician in New York City." **Available in Spanish as** *Un grillo en Times Square.* Yearling, 1999 (176p).

Van Allsburg, Chris. *Jumanji.* When Judy and Peter discover a mysterious board game in the park, a fantastic adventure begins—one that won't end until someone wins the game. **Also available in Spanish.** Houghton, 1981 (31p).

Vernon, Ursula. *Nurk.* Nurk the shrew lives a quiet life until he receives a letter asking for help and gets involved in finding a kidnapped dragonfly prince. Harcourt, 2008 (144p).

HISTORICAL FICTION

Armstrong, Jennifer. *Magnus at the Fire.* Magnus the horse and his team are retired from pulling a steam pumper when their firehouse gets its first fire engine, but Magnus won't be put out to pasture that easily. Simon & Schuster, 2005 (32p).

Borden, Louise. *The Greatest Skating Race.* Piet, a Dutch boy, takes on a dangerous mission: to escort two younger children to the safety of their aunt's house in Belgium during World War II. McElderry, 2004 (48p).

Casanova, Mary. *The Klipfish Code.* Marit and her brother are sent to live with their grandfather when the Nazis invade Norway, but Marit finds a way to help the resistance movement. Houghton, 2007 (240p).

Celenza, Anna Harwell. *Gershwin's Rhapsody in Blue.* A New York newspaper is advertising the upcoming debut of George Gershwin's new jazz concerto, but George hasn't composed it yet! Charlesbridge, 2006 (32p).

Kinsey-Warnock, Natalie. *Nora's Ark.* When torrential rain floods a Vermont river valley, Nora's grandparents welcome a host of neighbors into their unfinished house on a hill. HarperCollins, 2005 (32p).

Tingle, Tim. *Crossing Bok Chitto.* In pre-Civil War Mississippi, Martha, a Choctaw girl, begins a life-saving friendship with African American slaves across the river. Cinco Puntos, 2008 (40p).

INFORMATIONAL TEXT

Buckley, Annie and James Buckley, Jr. *Inside Photography.* The work of three active photographers—in fashion, news, and animal photography—is covered, highlighting attributes unique to each style. Child's World, 2007 (32p).

Claybourne, Anna. *Deep Oceans.* Covering methods of travel to the deep ocean and the life forms found there, this book speculates about how ocean exploration will change in the future. Heinemann, 2008 (48p).

Davies, Nicola. *Oceans and Seas.* The wonders of the sea, from its animals and plants to its tides and waves, are explained. Kingfisher, 2007 (48p).

Gaff, Jackie. *I Wonder Why Pine Trees Have Needles and Other Questions About Forests.* In a question-and-answer format, a broad scope of information about forests is covered. Kingfisher, 2007 (32p).

Graham, Ian. *The Best Book of Speed Machines.* Throughout history, people have designed vehicles to move ever faster. Kingfisher, 2008 (32p).

Harrison, David L. *Cave Detectives.* When a Missouri road crew uncovered a cave in 2001, scientists discovered evidence of several prehistoric species. Chronicle, 2007 (48p).

Hirschi, Ron. *Lions, Tigers, and Bears: Why Are Big Predators So Rare?* Large animals such as grizzly bears and killer whales are fierce predators, but environmental changes threaten their existence. Boyds Mills, 2007 (40p).

Hiscock, Bruce. *Ookpik: The Travels of a Snowy Owl.* Born in the Arctic, a young snowy owl must find a region with a more plentiful food supply. Boyds Mills, 2008 (30p).

Hodgkins, Fran. *The Whale Scientists.* Scientists are trying to learn why whales strand themselves on beaches when death is the usual result. Houghton, 2007 (64p).

Hoena, B. A. *Shackleton and the Lost Antarctic Expedition.* This graphic novel is an account of Ernest Shackleton and his crew, who in 1907 escaped disaster on an attempt to reach the South Pole. Capstone, 2006 (32p).

Howard, Amanda. *Robbery File: The Museum Heist.* Thieves who stole two paintings from Amsterdam's Van Gogh Museum in 2002 left behind clues, which scientists studied using forensic techniques to solve the crime. Bearport, 2008 (32p).

Jenkins, Steve. *Living Color.* The wide range of color in the animal world serves many purposes, from evading predators to attracting a mate. Houghton, 2007 (32p).

Kurlansky, Mark. *The Cod's Tale.* This is the story of how the humble codfish helped shape the history of the world. Putnam, 2001 (48p).

Suggested Trade Book Titles • **123**

Literature Discussion

Lewin, Ted. *Tooth and Claw: Animal Adventures in the Wild.* The author relates some of his wildest animal encounters. HarperCollins, 2003 (112p).

Marx, Trish. *Steel Drumming at the Apollo.* A boys' steel drum band from Schenectady, New York, takes its talents to the Apollo Theater in New York City. Lee & Low, 2007 (56p).

Price, Sean. *Smokestacks and Spinning Jennys.* Beginning in the 1760s, the rapid replacement of manual work with machines initiated the Industrial Revolution. Raintree, 2007 (32p).

Quigley, Mary. *Mesa Verde.* Scientists have made surprising discoveries in their excavation of Mesa Verde. Heinemann, 2005 (48p).

Raczka, Bob. *Here's Looking at Me.* Since 1484, artists' self-portraits have revealed many clues about how they think of themselves. Millbrook, 2006 (32p).

Reynolds, Jan. *Frozen Land.* The Inuit continue to pass down their traditions, even as outside influences change their culture. Lee & Low, 2007 (32p).

Schulman, Janet. *Pale Male: Citizen Hawk of New York City.* A red-tailed hawk and his mate rear twenty-three chicks over a nine-year period on a Fifth Avenue apartment building, winning both enemies and champions in the process. Knopf, 2008 (40p).

Sitarski, Anita. *Cold Light: Creatures, Discoveries, and Inventions That Glow.* For hundreds of years people have been intrigued by animals and things that glow—something every firefly chaser can relate to. Boyds Mills, 2007 (48p).

Spilsbury, Richard. *Cartoons and Animation.* Animation has changed a great deal since its earliest years; an overview of contemporary techniques and career possibilities is presented. Heinemann, 2008 (56p).

Wechsler, Doug. *Frog Heaven: Ecology of a Vernal Pool.* Over the course of one year, a vernal pool in Delaware supports a rich variety of animal and plant life. Boyds Mills, 2006 (48p).

Whipple, Heather. *Hillary and Norgay.* Since Edmund Hillary and Tenzing Norgay first reached the top of the highest mountain in the world in 1953, mountain climbing has never been the same. Crabtree, 2007 (32p).

Wilkes, Angela. *The Best Book of Ballet.* All aspects of ballet are explained, from basic dance positions to acting in a performance. Kingfisher, 2007 (32p).

MYSTERY

Dowd, Siobhan. *The London Eye Mystery.* When Ted and Katrina's visiting cousin, Salim, boards a London tourist ride but doesn't disembark, the two must race against time to find out what happened. Fickling, 2008 (336p).

Konigsburg, E. L. *From the Mixed-Up Files of Mrs. Basil E. Frankweiler.* Claudia and her brother Jamie camp out in the Metropolitan Museum of Art, where they are caught up in a mystery involving a statue. Aladdin, 2007 (176p).

Nilsen, Anna. *The Great Art Scandal.* Readers must use clues to match 32 of the world's greatest artists to the paintings they created. **Available in Spanish as *El gran escándalo en el arte*.** Kingfisher, 2003 (48p).

Pinkwater, Daniel. *The Artsy Smartsy Club.* Nick, Loretta Fischetti, Bruno Ugg, and Henrietta (Nick's 6-foot-tall, 266-pound chicken) discover the sidewalk art of Lucy Casserole. HarperCollins, 2005 (165p).

Simon, Seymour. *Einstein Anderson, Science Detective: The Gigantic Ants and Other Cases.* Science whiz Einstein Anderson solves a variety of mysteries, including a snake that chases people and a machine that can stop hurricanes. Morrow, 1998 (165p).

POETRY

Brown, Calef. *Flamingos on the Roof.* Twenty-nine humorous, irresistible nonsense poems play with language. Houghton, 2006 (64p).

Carroll, Lewis. *Jabberwocky.* Carroll's classic poem is interpreted anew through the illustrations of Christopher Myers. Hyperion, 2007 (32p).

Florian, Douglas. *Comets, Stars, the Moon, and Mars.* Poems explore the universe in both its vastness and its intimate detail. Harcourt, 2007 (56p).

Grimes, Nikki. *Oh, Brother!* Twenty poems tell the story of two boys who adjust to becoming brothers when their parents marry. Amistad, 2007 (32p).

Lewis, J. Patrick. *Please Bury Me in the Library.* An array of poems in various forms celebrate libraries, books, and the joy of reading. Harcourt, 2005 (32p).

Mora, Pat. *Yum! ¡Mmmm! ¡Qué Rico!* The haiku in this collection celebrate foods that originated in the Americas. Lee & Low, 2007 (32p).

Shields, Carol. *Almost Late to School and More School Poems*. These school poems take many forms including a concrete poem, poems for two voices, and a jump rope rhyme. Puffin, 2005 (48p).

Sidman, Joyce. *Song of the Water Boatman and Other Pond Poems*. Each of these lyrical poems about pond life is accompanied by a brief paragraph elaborating on that poem's subject. Houghton, 2005 (32p).

REALISTIC FICTION

Blume, Judy. *Tales of a Fourth-Grade Nothing*. Peter finds that it's not easy being the older brother of a mischievous two-year-old. Puffin, 2007 (128p).

Blume, Lesley M. M. *Cornelia and the Audacious Escapades of the Somerset Sisters*. Cornelia is beguiled by her new elderly neighbor, Virginia Somerset, through Virginia's captivating stories of her life. Yearling, 2008 (192p).

Cheng, Andrea. *Shanghai Messenger.* A Chinese American girl is invited to spend the summer in China with relatives she has never met. Lee & Low, 2005 (40p).

Danziger, Paula. *Amber Brown Goes Fourth.* Amber must start fourth grade as she copes with her parents' divorce and the fact that her best friend moved away. **Available in Spanish as *Ámbar en su cuarto y sin su amigo.* Puffin, 2007 (112p).

DeGross, Monalisa. *Donavan's Double Trouble.* Donavan's struggles in fourth grade include his math class and his beloved Uncle Vic, who has returned from overseas combat in a wheelchair. Amistad, 2007 (192p).

Frazee, Marla. *A Couple of Boys Have the Best Week Ever.* James and Eamon spend a week at Nature Camp, but exploring nature isn't nearly as interesting as doing indoor activities. Harcourt, 2008 (40p).

Greene, Stephanie. *Sophie Hartley, on Strike.* Sophie learns that going on strike to protest her housekeeping chores only creates more problems. Clarion, 2006 (160p).

Hannigan, Katherine. *Ida B.* Fun-loving, home-schooled Ida B must face public school and other changes when her mother becomes seriously ill. **Available in Spanish as *Ida B: . . . y sus planes para potenciar el diversión, evitar desastres y (posiblemente) salvar al mundo.*** HarperCollins, 2006 (256p).

Kyi, Tanya Lloyd. *Jared Lester, Fifth-Grade Jester.* Jared knows his fantasy of becoming a court jester is far-fetched, until he learns that the Queen will be passing through town. Annick, 2006 (74p).

Lin, Grace. *The Year of the Dog.* Pacy hopes to "find herself" as the Chinese Year of the Dog begins. Little, Brown, 2007 (160p).

Lombard, Jenny. *Drita, My Homegirl.* Maxine, a popular fourth-grader, befriends Drita, the new girl from Kosovo. Puffin, 2006 (144p).

Mills, Claudia. *Being Teddy Roosevelt.* Inspired by the perseverance of Teddy Roosevelt, whom he is studying for a school project, Riley is determined to find a way to acquire a saxophone. Farrar, 2007 (96p).

Paterson, Nancy Ruth. *The Winner's Walk.* Case warms quickly to a dog that follows him home one day, but when he learns that it was trained to help a girl with disabilities, he must decide what to do. Farrar, 2006 (128p).

Ransom, Candice. *Seeing Sky-Blue Pink.* Maddie isn't sure whether she can trust her new stepfather or whether she'll like living in the country. Carolrhoda, 2007 (122p).

Smith, Charles R., Jr. *Winning Words: Sport Stories and Photographs.* Quotations and stories about overcoming fears and trying one's hardest are presented. Candlewick, 2008 (80p).

Tate, Lindsey. *Kate Larkin, the Bone Expert.* Recovering from an injury gives curious Kate an opportunity to learn about the science of broken bones. Holt, 2008 (64p).

Urban, Linda. *A Crooked Kind of Perfect.* Zoe dreams of playing the piano, but her parents buy her an organ instead, and soon she's practicing for the Perform-O-Rama organ competition. Harcourt, 2007 (214p).

TRADITIONAL TALE

Babbitt, Natalie. *Jack Plank Tells Tales.* In a boarding house run by Nina's mother, the residents try to help find a new job for Jack Plank, a pirate who doesn't plunder well and has recently been sacked. Michael di Capua, 2007 (144p).

Giovanni, Nikki. *The Grasshopper's Song.* In this twist on an Aesop fable, Jimmy Grasshopper sues the Ants for failing to appreciate his artistic endeavors. Candlewick, 2008 (56p).

Johnson, Paul Brett. *Fearless Jack.* In this Appalachian folktale, Jack wins fame and fortune after killing ten yellow jackets with one whack. Margaret K. McElderry, 2001 (32p).

Kellogg, Steven. *Sally Ann Thunder Ann Whirlwind Crockett.* Sally Ann, wife of Davy Crockett, fears nothing—and proves it when braggart Mike Fink tries to scare her. William Morrow, 1995 (48p).

Mosel, Arlene. *Tikki Tikki Tembo.* This Chinese folktale tells the story of a boy whose long name gets in the way of his rescue from a well. Henry Holt, 1968 (32p).

Nolen, Jerdine. *Hewitt Anderson's Great Big Life.* Tiny Hewitt, the son of giants, finds a way to ease his parents' worries about his small size. Simon & Schuster, 2005 (40p).

Professional Bibliography

Barrentine, Shelley. "Engaging with reading through interactive read-alouds." *The Reading Teacher, 50(1):* 36–43.

Clay, Marie M. *Becoming Literate: The Construction of Inner Control.* Heinemann, 1991.

Clay, Marie M. *Change Over Time in Children's Literacy Development.* Heinemann, 2001.

Fountas, Irene. C. and G. S. Pinnell. *Guided Reading: Good First Teaching for All Children.* Heinemann, 1996.

Fountas, Irene C. and G. S. Pinnell. *Guiding Readers and Writers: Teaching Comprehension, Genre, and Content Literacy.* Heinemann, 2001.

Fountas, Irene C. and G. S. Pinnell. *Leveled Books, K–8: Matching Texts to Readers for Effective Teaching.* Heinemann, 2005.

Fountas, Irene C. and G. S. Pinnell. *Teaching for Comprehending and Fluency: Thinking, Talking, and Writing About Reading, K–8.* Heinemann, 2006.

Holdaway, Don. *The Foundations of Literacy.* Ashton Scholastic, 1979 (also Heinemann).

Pinnell, Gay Su and Irene C. Fountas. *The Continuum of Literacy Learning, Grades K–8: Behaviors and Understandings to Notice, Teach, and Support.* Heinemann, 2007.

Teacher's Notes

Teacher's Notes

Teacher's Notes

Teacher's Notes